MILITARY MAN
FAMILY MAN

Brassey's titles of related interest

DIETZ
Ten British Military Towns

SEGAL & SINAIKO
Life in the Rank and File

NAPIER
Brassey's Armed Services Careers Yearbook

BOWMAN
The All-Volunteer Force After a Decade

SWEETMAN
Sword and Mace

EDMONDS
The Defence Equation

MILITARY MAN
FAMILY MAN

by

RUTH JOLLY

BRASSEY'S DEFENCE PUBLISHERS
(a member of the Pergamon Group)

LONDON · OXFORD · WASHINGTON · NEW YORK · BEIJING
FRANKFURT · SÃO PAULO · SYDNEY · TOKYO · TORONTO

U.K. (Editorial)	Brassey's Defence Publishers, 24 Gray's Inn Road, London WC1X 8HR
(Orders)	Brassey's Defence Publishers, Headington Hill Hall, Oxford OX3 0BW, England
U.S.A. (Editorial)	Pergamon-Brassey's International Defense Publishers, 8000 Westpark Drive, Fourth Floor, McLean, Virginia 22102, U.S.A
(Orders)	Pergamon Press, Maxwell House, Fairview Park, Elmsford, New York 10523, U.S.A.
PEOPLE'S REPUBLIC OF CHINA	Pergamon Press, Room 4037, Qianmen Hotel, Beijing, People's Republic of China
FEDERAL REPUBLIC OF GERMANY	Pergamon Press, Hammerweg 6, D-6242 Kronberg, Federal Republic of Germany
BRAZIL	Pergamon Editoria, Rua Eça de Queiros, 346, CEP 04011, Paraiso, São Paulo, Brazil
AUSTRALIA	Pergamon-Brassey's Defence Publishers, P.O. Box 544, Potts Point, N.S.W. 2011, Australia
JAPAN	Pergamon Press, 8th Floor, Matsuoka Central Building, 1-7-1 Nishishinjuku, Shinjuku-ku, Tokyo 160, Japan
CANADA	Pergamon Press Canada, Suite No. 271, 253 College, Street, Toronto, Ontario, Canada M5T 1R5

Copyright © 1987 Ruth Jolly

First English Language Edition 1987

Library of Congress Cataloging-in-Publication Data

Jolly, Ruth A.
Military man, family man.
1. Soldiers—Great Britain—Family relationships.
2. Military social work—Great Britain.   3. Sociology, Military—Great Britain. I. Title.
UB405.G7J64   1987   306'.27'0941   87–14772
ISBN 0–08–031204–7

British Library Cataloguing in Publication Data

Jolly, Ruth A.
Military man, family man, crown property?
1. Great Britain. *Army*—Military life
2. Soldiers—Great Britain—Family relationships
I. Title
355.1'0941   U767
ISBN 0–08–031204–7

Printed in Great Britain by
Richard Clay Ltd, Bungay, Suffolk

Contents

Preface

This book has arisen from my dual interest in the military and in sociology. As a former WRAF Officer and as a military wife with children I have experienced many aspects of the military way of life—some enjoyable, some infuriating. As a student of social studies and a practising social worker, the complex communities of Servicemen and their families seem to me endlessly fascinating, but I have been struck by how little many of my professional friends and colleagues really know about the peculiar lifestyle of a 'Service family'. The days when most men had seen voluntary or conscripted military service are long past and today the military is a foreign world to a great number of people. The way that world looks now, and ways in which it is changing, form the subject matter of the book.

Interviews and case studies gathered during the year 1985 constitute a vital part of the text. My subjects and I met in one of three ways. In some instances, I went to military units as an 'official' visitor with a prearranged programme and a series of interviews and discussions organised for me at my request. In other instances, I visited units informally, staying with friends and talking to as many people as possible in the setting of their own homes. Finally, I was put in touch with some people whose case histories were of particular relevance to the book through friends and through professional colleagues. I have unashamedly made use of personal contacts; without them this book could never have been written.

In order to preserve the anonymity of my interviewees, I have changed their names and some of their personal details. Interviews were, in the main, recorded in note form during the course of discussion. This I found to be the method least threatening to my subjects and most suited to my own style of working. Having said this, some interviews were tape-recorded, and a very few were the result of informal conversations in a social setting, written down at the earliest possible moment.

General interviews were structured according to the formats given at the end of the book. However, although interviewees responded to the whole range of topics outlined, I allowed them to talk at length about points which clearly interested them, covering other facets of the discussion more briefly.

Two further issues should also be mentioned. Firstly, I would like to make the point that I realise there is a small but growing number of military women who are also family women. Their situation is certainly worthy of study, but since their numbers are as yet too small to make a significant impact upon the armed forces, I have left them outside the scope of the present work.

The second issue is that of diversity, both between and within the three Armed Services. I have used the term 'miltary' to embrace the Army, the Navy and the RAF and have written about matters common to them all. In doing so, I have tried to avoid creating the impression that military men and their families form a homogeneous group; for they do not. Military communities are composed of a wide and rich variety of individuals whose social backgrounds, educational attainments, professional abilities, opinions, tastes and outlooks on life differ. Add to this the fact that each Service has its own social and organisational quirks and one can safely say that for every general statement about military life there will be at least one individual to whom it does not apply. As it is impossible to eradicate generalisation—implicit or explicit—from a book of this nature, I here and now extend my apologies to exceptional individuals, and entreat the reader to view any generalisations with a degree of caution.

I hope this book will interest Servicemen and their families and will provoke discussion in military circles. Moreover, I believe that some of the content has relevance for allied groups, such as the Police Force, the Diplomatic Service and their families. In addition, my intention has been to write for members of the 'helping professions' (doctors, health visitors, teachers, social workers, probation officers etc.) who may find themselves working with military communities they only partially understand. I hope that any such readers will find this book useful.

RAJ

Acknowledgements

I would like to express my thanks to all those who gave their time to talk to me in the course of this investigation.

I am especially grateful to those who contributed not only opinions, but ideas, information and contacts; to Capt. A. J. Oglesby, OBE, M.Phil, MIPM, RN, now Deputy Controller (Services Support), SSAFA, to Mr C. F. H. Jessup, MA Senior Lecturer, University of Bristol, to Dr B. T. Dodd, Principal Psychologist, Ministry of Defence, to Lieutenant Colonel R. N. D. Hornby, RA and to Lady Elizabeth Kitson. In addition, I am particularly indebted to Air Vice Marshal R. A. Mason, CBE, MA, RAF, for all his help and encouragement during the early stages of the project.

My thanks are also due to the Ministry of Defence for permitting me to visit military bases and to talk to serving personnel. Although the resulting book in no way reflects 'official' views, I hope it will be seen as sympathetic to the military and constructive in outlook.

Finally, having written about numerous military families, I must thank my own—my husband, Peter, and children Sarah, Tim and Charles. Their patience, interest and good-humoured support were invaluable.

*   *   *

CHAPTER 1

The Military Man in a Changing Society

The Military Inheritance

The military as we know it today was born of the British Empire. Before that time, the Crown raised forces when necessary and paid them off again as quickly as possible. In peacetime, permanent soldiers were few in number, serving mainly to guard the monarch. But as the Empire began to take shape and expand during the late 17th and the 18th century, it became clear that neither the home-based militia nor the last-minute arrangement of commissioning ships and crews to form a navy was in any way adequate to meet a growing need to fight for supremacy at sea or to garrison territorial additions on the other side of the world. Thus, gradually, a sizeable professional standing Army and Navy came into being.

Regiments and ships were scattered in small depots throughout the Empire where they fought chiefly in minor skirmishes and short campaigns. As the greater part of the military was deployed overseas, it is not surprising that units developed an independent spirit and, marooned in alien societies, looked fiercely inward to maintain standards, morale and discipline. Being a long way from home most of the time, the professional military man was also outside the mainstream of social and political life in Britain. The military historian Correlli Barnett observed that '*The Army and the Nation had little to do with each other. . . .*'[1]

The tight world of the Victorian regiment or the ship's company was harsh and often wretched, but there also existed amongst the men a sense of belonging and a vehement loyalty to each other and to their Regiment or to their Ship. Commanding Officers, in their turn, generally took a paternalistic, if stern, interest in the conduct and morale of their men. Women and children featured on the fringes of this. Until the mid 19th century, unruly hoards of camp followers accompanied the troops everywhere; they included legal and common-law wives, prostitutes, cooks, seamstresses, washerwomen and so forth. In a reforming drive beginning after the Crimean War, the military authorities recruited manpower to perform many of the support tasks which had previously been undertaken by camp followers, and they began to extend to legitimate wives and children the

1

paternalistic concern which had hitherto been reserved for their menfolk.

Though change was more marked in the Army, the Navy too, began to distance itself from the motley band of hangers-on in the home ports and to give assistance and social recognition to sailors' wives and children. In the latter half of the 19th century, numbers of charitable trusts sprang up to give aid to soldiers' and sailors' dependants, who were seen as prime examples of 'the deserving poor'. The biggest and eventually best organised of these was the Soldiers' and Sailors' Families Association (now SSAFA), which was founded in 1885 to dispense financial relief, to encourage self-help and to put the case to the authorities for better pay and conditions within the Services. By the turn of the century, enlisted men could no longer truthfully be called 'the scum of the earth'; a reforming bureaucracy had ensured that they were basically trained, equipped and regularly paid and that their officially recognised dependants did not face destitution when the men went off to war.

As the military began to assume some responsibility for families, haphazard arrangements for accommodating them gave way to more standardised procedures. It became routine practice to allow numbers of wives and children to join their menfolk on long tours of duty in distant parts of the Empire. As time went by, this kind of provision was extended, until the military base-camp, at home and abroad, regularly came to include facilities not only for its men, but also some housing, schooling and medical services for families. By the time of the First World War, a 'respectable' family life had become an asset to a Serviceman's career. It demonstrated his qualities of dependability, his good, conventional morality and his fitness for promotion to greater authority over his fellows.

Once accommodation for families was available, the Commanding Officer's wife took her place at the top of the social pyramid of wives—and in the same way as her husband would, ideally, know all his men, she would know all their wives. Their lives were both protected and restricted by their military environment. Myna Trustram, in her book *Women of the Regiment*,[2] quotes an Army chaplain of the period speaking about the lot of the soldier's wife: '*As soon as the [marriage] knot is tied, she becomes an institution. She is part of the regiment and has a recognised rank in it . . .*' Dr Trustrum continues:

> '*And so the system of military marriage absorbed women and children into the hierarchy of the regiment. The threat posed by family ties to a man's military efficiency could be minimised by placing the whole family under army discipline. . . . In return for granting women and children certain welfare provisions the army could regulate families' lives and demand a certain kind of behaviour from them. These provisions were not seen as rights but were referred to as "privileges" and "indulgences" with the implication that families should be grateful for them. Women who broke the regimental rules risked being struck off the strength and hence being denied these "privileges".*'

Between the two World Wars, more houses and better houses were built—some at quite remote bases—and at a time of economic depression, the families of Servicemen enjoyed security and a decent standard of living. The calibre of men joining the Armed Forces rose higher than ever before and the image of extreme disreputability was finally laid to rest.

The years 1939–1945 involved the whole population in an unprecedented war effort and huge sums of money were spent on the Services. Afterwards, those who remained and those who joined as young men found themselves in a relatively privileged group. British military communities were scattered all over the globe, in some cases fighting, in some cases simply maintaining a 'presence' while politicians negotiated the gradual, final, winding-down of Empire. Against a background of post-war austerity, military men and their families though not affluent, were comfortable. They benefitted from such perquisites as cheap housing, NAAFI supplies of foodstuffs and drink at protected prices, batting (personal servants) for officers and their families and a very high standard of living indeed overseas. Military units were still fairly small and at least semi-autonomous. A Squadron Leader still commanded a squadron, a Leading Seaman still had subordinates to lead. The Serviceman's world remained tightly-knit and inward-looking—self-consciously different from 'civvy street'.

But times were changing, British colonies achieved independence and the military steadily withdrew from more and more overseas bases. In the space of under two decades, territories which had formed the backdrop to generations of Servicemen's lives, suddenly became foreign countries where they had no business to be. Beginning with India and Pakistan (granted independence in 1947) the military wound up its affairs and pulled out, repeating the process in Burma and Palestine, the Persian Gulf, Malaya and then the African countries of Ghana, Nigeria, Sierra Leone, Tanganyika, Uganda and Kenya.

In April 1949, NATO came into being and for the first time in centuries, the British military mind in peacetime was focussed on European matters. In 1957 Mr Duncan Sandys, the Minister of Defence, presented a Defence White Paper which plotted the future shape of British defence forces. The wartime expedient of National Service was to be abolished and the new, peacetime military was to be a small, élite force of highly-trained regular Servicemen.

By 1960, nobody thought of the British military as an imperial force, but its long years of being exactly that left an enduring legacy. That legacy can be described in terms of a British military outlook—an outlook which has been preserved and passed on to succeeding generations of serving men who have been taught their craft by British officers. It is characterised first by an unshakable commitment to professionalism—and a shuddering distaste for the concept of conscription or citizen soldiers (a militia such as exists in Sweden or Switzerland). Secondly, it is manifested in a fierce defence of the importance of detachment and distance from the rest of society: the military as a breed apart. *Of* society but not *in* it; apolitical, traditionalist, self-contained. These were virtues born of necessity in the days of Empire, but are tenets harder to maintain in a military which is now based firmly on our own shores.

Correlli Barnett, writing in 1970 said:

> '*The Empire has disintegrated, the British global role has been packed up, British national policy is to be concentrated on Europe. We stand, it cannot be too strongly emphasised, at one of the great turning-points of our history, when a cycle of three hundred years of expansion and contraction is coming to an end. It is to be wondered how far the implications of this have sunk in—to politicians, state-servants, servicemen, let alone the public at large. Marlborough's and Wellington's victories, the great eighteenth century sea-fights, mercantile expansion, the Industrial Revolution, world empire, world power—all of it is past. . . . For the Armed Forces, the consequences of this transformation, both strategic and social, must be immense.*'[3]

*   *   *

Husbands, Fathers and Families

A brief look at the military inheritance of today's Serviceman provides only half of the picture as far as the family man is concerned. For over the corresponding period, from the days of Empire until the present, the role of husbands and fathers in our society has undergone quite considerable change.

Tracing this process in broad terms, we must begin in the early days of Empire, the late 17th and early 18th centuries, when Britain was an agrarian society, certainly with thriving towns and a vigorous commercial life, but one in which the majority of the population worked on the land. The extended family, headed by a patriarch, was the social norm which, despite variation from the pattern (the sociologists Michael Young and Peter Willmott have amassed evidence to show that even before the Industrial Revolution, nuclear families living far away from their families of origin were not uncommon), endured well into the industrial 19th century.[4] Indeed, W. F. Ogburn, writing only some fifty years ago produced ample material to demonstrate that in some parts of rural Britain, this pre-industrial pattern of family functioning still existed, though precariously.

In agrarian Britain the 'typical' family was centred on the village or the hamlet. Settlers from outside were rare and for most families in a locality, the parish boundaries formed the practical limit of their world. Two or three generations of a family would live in the same village, would practise a craft such as smithying or tanning or would work on the land, and upon the shoulders of the working father would fall the ultimate burden of providing for his family. He taught his sons, and perhaps his nephews too, the skills they would need to earn a living themselves, and his wife and daughters plus any elderly dependant relatives, took on a supporting role. This in itself was demanding, involving the carrying out of both domestic tasks and also some economic activity, for example making butter or baskets for sale, spinning, taking in washing and so on.

Much has been written about the demise of the typical extended family, as industrialisation favoured the more flexible, more mobile nuclear family, divested of its obligations to a complex kinship network. But ideological change, that is, notions of how a family *ought* to operate, was very gradual. Although the economic independence of families disappeared when they moved into the industrial towns and working members sold their labour to big employers, close geographical and domestic links between relations were commonly retained. (This kind of family closeness is now only to be found in a few, traditionally working class mining and industrial areas, and even here, it is a way of life that is in decline.) The change of father's work place from the home environment to the factory or office undermined his teaching function in respect of his offspring but reinforced his role as worker.

By the beginning of the 20th century, the 'typical' working man was a town dweller and the ideology of the nuclear family had gained cultural acceptance. The term 'family' had ordinarily come to refer to that social unit which comprised a mother and a father bound by marriage, their children and possibly a dependant relative, living under one roof. The extended family, with its wide kinship interdependence, had diminished in importance. Industrial society called for individual achievement and mobility, and the older family and neighbourhood networks of support for the disabled, the sick, the children and the elderly were gradually, falteringly, replaced by charitable schemes, self-help groups and finally, by state relief.

The kind of family functioning which was then the norm would be described today as 'traditional'. The husband and wife carried out distinct and quite different roles. The husband was breadwinner, and because the income and social status of his family rested very largely upon his performance in the job market, family considerations had to take second place to the support of the man of the house and his job. This applied whether the man was a miner or factory worker, whose wife would endeavour to ensure for him good food, clothing and time off with his friends in order that he should remain a reasonable provider for the family—or a wealthy business man, whose wife would be by his side at society functions, would entertain the 'right' people and who would, on his behalf, organise the servants of his household. If a wife had a job it was almost certainly because her family could not survive without her income; moreover it would be low-paid, low-status 'women's work'—millhand or cook, shop assistant or dressmaker. ... The working mother with a professional occupation was, to all intents and purposes, unheard of. A wife's primary task was the running of the home and the care of the children.

Childhood, too, was viewed distinctively. It is said that the Victorians 'invented' childhood. Perhaps it would be truer to say that they idealised it, sentimentalised it. One reason why this occurred is that with industrialisation, most fathers' occupations were removed from the home, and this served to distance them from the day-to-day upbringing of their children. By the same token, childhood—with domesticity—became cut off from the world of work, and the perceived ideal of childhood became cosy and domesticated, too. Although there was poverty and hardship in plenty for the children of the poor, all classes subscribed to a general notion of childhood as they felt it ought to be: a carefree, irresponsible time, a period in which training for later life should be unpressured, focussed on the home and the school and secluded from the harsher world of the factory or the pit, the bank or the boardroom.

Looking for an arbitrary date for the 'end' of the traditional industrial era, the Second World War can be viewed as one of the final acts of Britain as an advanced but already decaying industrial society. The 'technological age' (or post-industrial period, whatever the favoured terminology) was already beginning. By now, however, cultural acceptance of the traditional family roles which oiled the wheels of industrial society was well entrenched in the social consciousness of the people. But it was an ideology of the family which was now bound to a waning economic system, and as structural economic change occurred in post-war Britain, social change occurred also.

Ingredients of Change

It is interesting to note that, whilst changes at the time of the Industrial Revolution most directly affected the position of men, changes since the end of the Second World War have most directly affected the status of women and children.

One of the biggest of these changes has been the creation of the Welfare State. In Britain, moves towards state benefits for all citizens in need began in the 19th century, but it was not until the 1940s that a secure system of social care 'from the cradle to the grave' was finally constructed. The 1944 Education Act, the 1945 Family Allowances Act, the 1946 Industrial Injuries Act, the National Insurance Act of the same year and in 1948 the National Assistance Act, the Children's Act and finally, the National Health Act set up a framework of social security which, at that time, was the best in the world. As a result, families were no longer absolutely dependent upon the earning capacity of the father (possibly supplemented by the mother's wage) to ensure enough to eat, somewhere to live, clothes and shoes to wear and fuel to burn. Now, for the first time, an ordinary family without a father knew it could survive, adequately at least. A consequence of this has been an easing of the social stigma attached to those who, in previous times, would have been a burden to their relations—the unmarried mother, the divorcee, the widow. Although they are still to be found in disproportionate numbers amongst the poorest in our society, the state does at least ensure that they can live independently. This fact has undermined one of the basic functions of the traditional father—to build and maintain a satisfactory material standard of living for his family. Since, traditionally, this was never considered to be the mother's primary task, her position was not similarly undermined. It was, if anything, enhanced, as she now possessed a greater measure of independence from her husband.

On a different front, however, the traditional role of the wife has been undermined. Since the war, technological advance which was transforming industry, has entered the home. Labour-saving domestic appliances have completely altered the nature of housework. Keeping a home functioning no longer involves such tedious and back-breaking tasks as scrubbing the washing by hand, black-leading the kitchen range, carrying coals, carrying water and so on; neither does it require special skills which mothers used to pass on to their daughters slowly, throughout childhood: how to cook stew and dumplings, how to mend a shirt and turn a collar or how to starch and iron a ruff or a frill. The advent of household machinery from vacuum cleaners to washing machines, of easy-care fabrics and convenience foods has combined to undermine the status of the housewife. There remains no job around the house that a man cannot do and many that a child can tackle with a minimum of instruction. The domestic skills of the traditional housewife are obsolete.

Another traditional task—for more leisured women—was 'charitable works'. Here again, the Welfare State has taken care of many of the more challenging jobs. Social work has become a profession, with legal rights and duties, and the kindly, enthusiastic amateur has been largely relegated to the 'second division'. Fund-raising, ferrying people around, visiting the lonely, these are the important, but mundane tasks which are assigned to volunteers. On the whole, they are not sufficiently highly regarded to give a woman with no other occupation an abiding sense of personal worth.

But if the status of woman as a housewife has been undermined, her emergent status as a citizen in her own right has (in the view of most younger women, at any rate) more than compensated. For women have arrived on the labour market in force. Well over half of working-aged women in Britain are now in some form of employment.[5] The money they earn, the promotion they achieve, gives them a measure of power and influence both outside and within their homes that most of their great-grandmothers would have considered impossible. (And, no doubt, quite improper!)

Accounting for this massive influx of women into the world of work are three major factors. The first is that technological advances in industry have reduced the need for workers with muscle-power and increased numbers of lighter jobs in factories—particularly those producing high-tech consumer goods. Furthermore, numbers in the service occupations have multiplied and all manner of jobs in this sector have opened up; jobs which competent women can perform as well as competent men. Even allowing for current unemployment problems, there is work around for women to do.

A second factor is that owing to the invention, manufacture and general availability of efficient contraceptive devices, more women are actually available for work. Women can now control their own fertility, and nowadays they do not spend the greater part of their most vigorous years in bearing and raising children. Nevertheless, many do seek alternative outlets for their talents and energies, and the market-place can often use their abilities.

A third factor is that women are, or can be, as well trained as men for today's competitive search for satisfying employment. State education ensures the same access to the same education for boys and for girls, and now that job opportunities for women are expanding, schoolgirls, as well as boys, think in terms of a career. Steadily, the number of girls taking '16 +' and 'A' level examinations, degree courses and professional qualifications, increases. Thus, more women are better equipped to enter a wider range of occupations than ever before.

The evolving technological society has also brought change to childhood. Once remote from the world of work, the need of a high-tech society for a skilled work-force and the rich rewards to be gained from becoming part of it make the formal education of children a matter crucial to their success in later life. As technical and service occupations demand ever higher levels of academic qualification for entry and advancement, children of both sexes and from a wide range of social backgrounds have to work hard from an early age to pass examinations. It is difficult, it is competitive. More young people than ever hold paper qualifications, but scientific advance and anxious employers relentlessly raise standards. Education has become a serious matter for parents seeking the best possible start in life for their children. What is more, by the time they leave school, many, if not most, children know more than their parents about a number of subjects. Computers, mathematics, languages—all are fields in which many children can out-perform their parents. This means that although their earning power, and thus their economic independence, is somewhat delayed, in relation to their industrial-era counterparts, their 'training' for work (though not for a specific job) begins at an increasingly early age. The importance of primary school attainment, for instance, is well recognised as an indicator of eventual scholastic success. Therefore, schooling is taken more seriously by modern parents and, to a certain extent, perhaps by children themselves, too. Parents respect their capacity to learn, to adapt, to re-learn and the knowledge which children possess and their parents lack is admired. Children are once again moving closer to the adult world.

Another factor which has greatly contributed to this move has been television. Television heads the league-table of family recreation and though several surveys have shown that children watch a good deal of Children's Television, they have also indicated that most of their *favourite* programmes are produced for adult audiences. Police-dramas, sport and soap operas are enormously popular with adults and children alike. Moreover, for more thoughtful children, access to the scene of current affairs through the medium of news programmes is as immediate for them as it is for their parents. Video reports of wars, disasters and demonstrations are familiar to today's children and details of sex-scandals and murder cases cannot be hidden from them. Children do not live a sheltered existence. They are physically healthier and materially far better off than their predecessors, but the preoccupations of the adult world impinge on their lives at a generally earlier age. The Victorian ideal of a childhood apart is no longer feasible, whatever parents may think they want.

The Symmetrical Family

Economic and technological change has strained the traditional ways of family functioning to a point where, in practice, few families actually reflect the traditional ideal in their own organisation.

> '*Families seem to be besieged from all sides. Divorce rates are climbing, marriage is being postponed, fertility rates are falling; increasing numbers of children are being raised only by their mothers, either because of divorce or because their parents were never married; and housewives in record numbers are rushing out of the home and into the labour market.*'[6]

Some sociologists have questioned whether the family as we know it will survive. Feminists, too, have not been slow to point out the steady erosion of the conventional paternal role and to express doubts as to whether families need fathers around at all. But in spite of this, it seems that people still want to marry and that married couples still desire children. Marriage and remarriage rates are high and couples remaining voluntarily childless are unusual. So despite the lack of long term success in one third of marriages in Britain today, the ideal of a lifetime's partnership and the creation of a stable family persists.

If the ideal of family stability has not really altered, what *is* changing is the way in which married couples are viewing the organisational means to this end. The traditional image of the family (working father, domesticated mother and carefree, rosy-cheeked children) has receded to the make-believe world of breakfast cereal and soap-powder advertisements. Taking its place is an ideal which Michael Young and Peter Willmott have described as 'the symmetrical family'. This term refers to the nuclear family, conventional in composition (father, mother and children) but not in its assignment of roles. In the symmetrical family, the tasks of one parent are mirrored (not necessarily exactly) by the other, and also, to some degree, by the children. For instance, the father works outside the home—full or part-time—the mother does too; and their children, who are at school, are treated as students, working for their futures. The mother undertakes routine household chores, the father does also—so too, to a lesser extent, do the children. Few, if any, couples would share all tasks equally, but the keynote of the symmetrical *ideal* is that each parent, and the children, should be able to contribute something to all aspects of family life.

In 1971, when Rhona and Robert Rapoport published their book, *Dual Career Families*,[7] real-live families who worked in a highly symmetrical fashion were rare. (These were families where the mother's status at work and hours of work were broadly similar to her husband's.) Since then, dual-career families have become more common, but it is still unusual for a mother to continue working throughout the infancy of her children. However, as children grow older, more mothers resume employment.

The other important aspect of symmetry in families is the wider role of modern fathers in the upbringing of their children. We may wonder why this should have occurred. Are they becoming 'soft', feminised? Not so! Although one very good reason is that of simple enjoyment, there are in addition, significant social advantages which an 'involved' father can pass on to his offspring. Fathers who have careers rather than casual jobs (and this includes most military men) tend to belong to the growing sector of the skilled worker. Often their skills are very specialised and could certainly not be directly passed on to their children. However, the transmission of *cultural* know-how is a different matter. The scholar A. H. Halsey puts it thus:

> '*Cultural capital is of increasing importance. It is affirmed and publicly recognised in degrees, certificates and credentials. And it is acquired first and foremost through familial transmission—for example, through knowledge of how to use the public properties of libraries and museums, through elaborated language codes which are indespensible for success at school, through appropriate levels of academic inspiration reinforced in the home, through information about learning or job opportunities.*'[8]

Of course, mothers play a large role in the conveying of 'cultural capital' to their children, but in our highly specialised, highly competitive society, the father who can add an extra dimension of information-giving and interest, can give his children abilities which will enable them in their turn to compete for posts in lucrative and interesting walks of life. More and more fathers are participating in this way—right from the beginning.

During the 1970s, as hospitals began to bow to pressure from expectant parents and allowed fathers to be present at the birth of their children, a rapidly increasing number did so. Fears that they might become over-anxious or increase the risk of infection proved unfounded, and now fathers are seldom excluded from the birth process. Traditionally, fathers took very little part in the care of their new-born infants. Men struggling with nappy pins and feeding bottles were the stuff of situation comedy, but recent studies (such as those described by Ross Parke in his book, *Fathering*) point to the fact that most present-day fathers have a close emotional bond with their infants, spend a significant amount of time in play with them and are highly competent care-givers. Of course, the amount of interest which men show in their children varies considerably from family to family, but Dr Parke is firm in his opinion that: *'Fathers are interacting much more with their infants than in the past.*[9] As with involvement in infancy, so also with the later stages of children's development. There is ample evidence to show that fathers from a wide cross-section of society regularly participate in practical ways in the early socialisation of their children.* Today's fathers are to be seen pushing prams, visiting play-parks, taking children to school and, as any primary school teacher will attest, taking a formidable interest in early progress. A First-School Head remarked:

> *'Fifteen or twenty years ago open evenings in the infant school were attended, if at all, by mother. Nowadays, we get both parents, and fathers don't just come as spectators; they know all about the reading and maths schemes their children are doing and they ask pretty searching questions about progress. . . . Another change too is that nowadays we're seeing a lot of dads at things like the Christmas Nativity play and the end of term entertainments . . .'*

The journalist Maureen Green makes the point:

> *'If a father starts early to take an interest in the books and television programmes, the games and crazes of his children's age-group—and the child's cultural milieu shifts very rapidly—he can also make sure that his children learn from the beginning about what interests him, the music and books and sport that a grown-up prefers.'*[10]

The sort of father who can play a major role in initiating his children into the complex culture of present-day society, gives them an advantage in the race to accumulate that precious 'cultural capital' which will help them to acquire social and material status as adults.

Fathers are needed by their children—for play, for emotional security and for help in mastering 'the system'. But fathers also need their families, and not just so that they can feel useful, but for their own emotional stability. Stress has become a factor in most demanding jobs: the pace of life, the pace of change, the need for accuracy, the competition for advancement; all these things make the world of work a far less predictable place than it used to be. It is frequently the case that the higher the stress-factor in a job, the more important a home and family becomes to a man. For here, he can relax and be truly himself; here he does not have to prove his cost-effectiveness or build his image. Jacques Grandmaison succinctly describes the family as: *'a locus of personal identity in an uncertain world.'*[11]

*Some interesting work in this field is listed under the section headed 'Recommended for Further Reading'.

Leonard Benson concludes: '*An important function of the family is to guarantee the highly-skilled male a sense of inter-personal security.*'[12]

Families need fathers; fathers need families.

*   *   *

Military Man, Family Man

Symmetrical families, 'involved' fathers, high-tech, high-stress occupations. Where does all this leave the military man? Well . . . more often than not in Belize or Belfast, Port Stanley or Portsmouth, moving intermittently in and out of the mainstream of his family life.

The young man who joins the military is the product of a post-war upbringing, and is going to share the views which predominate amongst his generation concerning marriage and the family. If he is well educated (and a *majority* of entrants now have sixth form, adult education college or day-release courses behind them)[13] He is quite likely to take the view that marriage entails a sharing of responsibilities between partners—responsibilities for earning, for decision-making, for parenting. He may expect and want to play an active role in the rearing of his children. By the same token, his wife may expect and want to play an active role in the economic support of the family and to devote only a few years of her total life-span to the home-based care of children and their pre-school socialisation. But the military, for a husband and father, is not an occupation which comfortably allows for a sharing of family responsibilities. It is a way of life which is compatible with the older, traditional division of labour between the breadwinner husband and the housewife. And it is not very amenable to change, because the Serviceman *belongs* to the military and cannot ultimately decide how he wishes to divide his time and efforts between his job and his family. He is never truly off-duty, even on leave he must be contactable; his private life can be opened to the scrutiny of his superiors; he cannot refuse outright to go where he is sent, or to stay for as long as he is told. He cannot avoid long or unsocial hours of work, he cannot withdraw his labour. This is not to say that his job-satisfaction is low (in fact, the reverse is more usually the case) but that the Serviceman's final lack of control over his own hours of work, type of work and geographical place of work makes it very difficult for him to share in domestic responsibilities or for his wife to pursue a parallel career, with any degree of continuity.

Making this situation worse is the clear expectation of the Military Establishment that Service families will continue to run on traditional lines. None of this 'symmetrical family' nonsense! The military man is head of his household; his wife supports him and the military helps him to look after her and their children. In order to maintain the morale of the fighting forces, the Serviceman's family will, whenever possible, follow him from one posting to another, renting a married quarter on a housing estate which the Ministry of Defence has built on or near the military base. The base will have a social life of its own, presided over by the Commanding Officer and his wife, and whilst the ordinary Serviceman's wife will not be coerced into joining in, the Establishment will look favourably upon those who do. For military work is often difficult and dangerous, often unpleasant, and the maintenance of a cheerful community spirit *is* important. Servicemen's children are likewise expected to accompany their parents from one place to another, changing schools as they go, or if they are the offspring of 'officers and gentlemen', it is assumed that they will probably go to boarding school anyway. The military will, with paternalistic care, provide the best facilities for families which it can afford; but when families use them, they will still do so as 'Wife of —' or 'Child of —'. They are still dependants: they still have no entitlements of their own. The point is that the military man himself, secure in the knowledge that his family is provided for, should be able to leave home for long periods at a time, work unsocial hours, and keep his whole attention on the job in hand.

However, it isn't as simple as that: not any more. The whole concept for men of 'supporting a family' has shifted in emphasis. What was, traditionally, a financial and managerial role has become more markedly a position of emotional support and practical help, and here there is a paradox. The military is in the forefront of technological advance, requiring ever higher standards of knowledge and performance from its men in order to manage modern equipment. But it is a 'tail-ender' as far as social change is concerned. The result is the paradoxical expectation of the military that it will be able to recruit men who are up-to-standard for the job, have sufficient determination and initiative to succeed, and yet, in their private lives—their family lives—will be innately conservative and will adopt the social attitudes of an earlier generation. In fact, since the demands of the job come first, high-calibre candidates are recruited—the Services are choosy—and if a wildly unconforming attitude might bring rejection, a candidate with an intelligently questioning outlook is regarded favourably. So, as the military takes for itself an ever-larger proportion of the nation's better educated young men (and there are now private soldiers, naval ratings and airmen beginning technical careers in the military at the very bottom of the rank structure, who hold university degrees), it finds itself with quite a number of entrants whose social attitudes do not snugly fit those expected by the Military Establishment.

Furthermore, older men who have successfully negotiated huge technological change during the course of their careers are also likely to be able, intellectually flexible and quite receptive to changing ideas in all fields. This means that at all ranks, a significant proportion of Servicemen today do not go along unthinkingly with the 'party line' on the way in which military and family commitments will be dovetailed.

Change has crept into the military. People notice it, they record it, but they don't talk about it too much, lest they be considered disloyal. Nevertheless, the fact is that military families are rapidly becoming 'civilianised'. It began in earnest with a move amongst Servicemen to buy their own houses. Throughout the 1960s, house prices had risen and then, in the early 1970s, they rocketted. Military men leaving the forces after a full career were unable to afford to buy a decent property with their fixed gratuities. Inflation was cutting into the value of the serving man's pay and a mortgage on a house, for those who could afford it, made good financial sense. In 1970, they were helped by the introduction of the military salary. At its core was the decision of government to stop treating the armed forces as a perpetual 'special case'. Perks (such as they were by then) were to cease and anomalies whereby married and single men of the same rank and specialisation received different pay and allowances, would also cease. Henceforth, their jobs would be evaluated and, for pay purposes, would be equated with similar civilian occupations. An 'X' factor would be added to compensate for hardship, unsocial hours and so forth. In consequence, the disposable income of the Serviceman leapt to equivalent civilian rates, and many took this opportunity to buy into the housing market. Today, well over half of all married men in the Royal Navy own a house, around a half of married RAF personnel and around a quarter of married soldiers do so. Amongst all three Services, the percentage rises with age and income.[14] The military salary also had another effect, not so much practical as symbolic. It demonstrated that the government now viewed soldiers, sailors and airmen as citizens with special skills, not as special citizens.

In tandem with the trend towards house ownership, there has also been a steady increase in the numbers of men who, owning a home, are voluntarily serving unaccompanied in other parts of the UK—even overseas—rather than move their families.[15]

Two other factors which are making for a civilianisation of families are trends which also affect society at large. The first is the increase in numbers of working wives. Owing to reduced job opportunities for women who keep moving house every two years or so, the proportion of Service wives *seeking* work is higher than that amongst the rest of the community and the proportion *in work* is smaller. Having said that, around forty per cent of Service wives have a job. It seems that quite a lot of these women are not entirely happy with the kind of work which they are doing, and when they find a good job, they are reluctant to leave it when their husbands are posted out of the area. This applies particularly to professionally qualified women—of whom there now a significant number, mostly, though not exclusively, married to officers.[16]

The other factor is one which civilianises families 'at a stroke'—divorce.

Divorce rates in Britain have climbed steadily since the Divorce Reform Act of 1971 and one marriage in every three now ends this way.[17] The military maintains that its own divorce rate is no higher, and may even be a little lower, than that of society in general. This is very doubtful, military statistics are incomplete and inadequately produced. The statistician John Haskey[18] categorised all Decrees Absolute for the year 1979 in terms of social class, occupation, etc., and amongst his findings was the fact that, during *that particular year*, the Armed Forces suffered a higher divorce rate than any other occupation group. Obviously, the military is not keen to be viewed as a high risk occupation for divorce, but as interviews later in the book will bear out, this view is taken by many serving men and their wives.

The Armed Forces, whilst wholeheartedly embracing technological innovation, are reluctant to think about social change. What will happen to the fighting man's morale if families decamp and live their own independent lives away from the military bases? What will become of military communities in remote places if the only families who live there are the very young and the inadequate? If the military can no longer exercise control over families through financial or social pressure, how can it predict the ways in which they might influence their menfolk? If Servicemen become civilians and family men first and military men second, where would their loyalties lie in time of danger?

In view of these questions, perhaps we ought to ask whether we actually want family men in the military at all? Supposing there were options: single men only, or mercenaries from allied nations, would that solution give us a better deal? It might produce a more adventurous, positive force—men with no desire to head for home and babysit. Well, it might produce that, but such a force, even if filled with dedicated men (which would be unlikely) would surely not give us our best defenders. For, even if the family man experiences some conflict of loyalties in peacetime, we should still strive to keep him at the heart of our Armed Services. Why? Because the man who has the greatest stake in a society is the man who will most wisely and bravely defend it. Machiavelli, in the early 16th century, putting the case for a standing army drawn from the citizenry of the state, wrote:

> '*The arms by which a prince defends his possessions are either his own or else auxiliaries, or mixed. The mercenaries and auxiliaries are useless and dangerous, and if anyone supports his state by the arms of mercenaries, he will never stand firm or sure, as they are disunited, ambitious, without discipline, faithless, bold among friends, cowardly among enemies. They have no fear of God and keep no faith with men. Ruin is only deferred as long as assault is postponed; in peace you are despoiled by them, and in war by the enemy. The cause of this is that they have no love or other motive to keep them in the field beyond a trifling wage, which is not enough to make them ready to die for your. . . .*'[19]

If our society is to be defended, we must retain an efficient, credible fighting force. It is therefore important, not just to military men but to the whole of society, that our Armed Services should be as well-managed, as

CHAPTER 2

Young Men Going Places

Most new entrants to the military today are reasonably well educated, physically fit, well-motivated young men. Many do not join with the aim of making their service into a long-term career and are not highly ambitious to rise through the ranks. However, for men of ability, the opportunity is there. 'High flyers' constitute only a small proportion of total numbers in any age group, but young 'high flyers', in particular, are an important group to study. They are the men who, by dint of personality and intellect, will influence the outlook of others in the years to come. A significant number, spurred on by early success, will remain in the military for the greater part of their working lives, and a proportion of these will eventually rise to the highest ranks, where they will wield considerable power. It is, therefore, not only interesting but also quite important to ask some of our most able young military men and their wives how they view their chosen career and the lifestyle that accompanies it.

This chapter looks at some young couples at an early point in the military husband's career. *None of these couples is 'typical': none is ordinary.* According to superiors, all the men are seen as 'particularly promising' and 'likely to go places': they are, in short, the kind of young men the military wants to attract—and to keep.

In order to discover the attitudes and expectations of this latest generation of 'high flyers', a small sample of young people took part in a series of structured interviews (see Appendix I). Twenty-five couples formed the basis of the sample to which was added a further twenty-eight individuals—people who could not be interviewed with their partner because he or she was unavailable at the time. This gave an overall total of seventy-eight participants, drawn from twelve military bases. Conversations lasted from one to two hours and discussion centred on five main topics: individual, social and educational backgrounds; the image which the men had of themselves as soldiers, sailors or airmen and their career hopes; wives' jobs or careers; attitudes towards home and domesticity; and ideas about actual or prospective roles as parents.

From the original sample interviewed, six couples represent the group well. Each is, in fact, an amalgam of two very similar couples. (This helps to protect the anonymity of the people involved and facilitates quotation from a wider range of interviews.) The six, it is hoped, will give a good general picture of the kind of young entrants who are currently doing well in the military and who may, one day, rise to high rank.

*   *   *

A Collection of Interviews

Army Corporal Peter Stevens is twenty-six, his wife Karen is two years younger and they have a ten-month-old son, Alexander. Peter joined the Army straight from school, which he left after gaining six 'O' levels. Originally, he had planned to work in his father's business—a small garage—but when the time came he found the prospect dull and so decided to sign on for the shortest possible time in the Army. '*The idea was to see some life and have some fun before settling down to a steady job.*' That was almost ten years ago, and Peter is still in the Army.

For the last three of these years, he has been married to Karen. They met through friends when he was at home in the north of England, on leave. Like Peter, Karen left school after 'O' levels and, with five to her credit, she became a bank clerk. It was a job she enjoyed and one which she continued after her marriage, being able to transfer to her bank's branch office in Aldershot, where Peter was based. As with many other military couples, Peter and Karen's courtship was a whirlwind affair and Karen admits that she didn't really know what she was taking on when marrying into the Army. Peter is a keen soldier and enjoys life with his regiment, but already he and Karen are worrying about the lack of stability which the way of life entails for families. Peter entered the Army as a single man with the object of widening his own horizons. He had no altruistic thoughts of serving his country or even of becoming a career soldier. But now the Army is making him consider these things. His name has been mentioned as a possible candidate for a commission and he and Karen have begun to think hard about the prospect of a life in the Army. . . .

Derek Pearson is the same age as Peter and holds the rate of Petty Officer. Before joining the Navy, Derek was an apprentice with a firm of engineers: '*I drifted into the apprenticeship because everyone at home and at school thought it was a good idea. But I never really liked it. My dad had been in the Marines and I guess the Navy was at the back of my mind for a long time. One day I just walked into a recruiting office and that was that—I chucked the apprenticeship. All Hell was let loose at home! But they calmed down. They're quite proud of me now I think.*' Derek's family live on the outskirts of Plymouth where his father, who left the Royal Marines as a Senior Non-Commissioned Officer, works as a Floor Manager in a factory. Nearly two years ago Derek married Lesley, a lively twenty-two-year-old, who was then a Leading Wren.

Lesley comes from a comfortable home in the suburbs of London, where her father is a Tax Inspector for the Inland Revenue. She joined the WRNS within a year of leaving school, having first worked briefly in a jeweller's shop. She had hoped to learn the trade: '*But I was just counter-staff and there was no proper training at all. . . . One of my mates went into the Wrens from school; we talked—and I joined up.*'

Lesley left the Wrens on marriage and is now expecting a baby: '*I did think at first about staying in, but Derek went to join a ship at Portsmouth and we decided to make a home for ourselves there. I did clerical work in the Wrens, so when I came out, I took a good secretarial course—word processors and all that—and I've had "temping" jobs ever since. I shall stop a couple of months before the baby's due.*' Derek has already had one long spell at sea since their marriage, and Lesley is well aware of the fact that being a sailor's wife means having to stand on one's own feet. . . .

Simon Watkins, as a Senior Aircraftsman in the RAF, is junior to the first two men. At twenty-three, he is also younger. He joined the RAF three and a half years ago and, with eight 'O' levels and one 'A' level, he holds better academic qualifications than most airmen. Indeed, it could be argued that he is somewhat over-qualified for his rather humdrum job as a clerk in the general office of a busy station in East Anglia: '*I originally intended to do a course in Electronics at polytechnic, but I failed my Physics and Chemistry 'A' levels. . . . I was totally fed up. My dad* [a PE teacher at a comprehensive school] *was furious—well, a mixture of anger and disappointment really. Now I can see I took the wrong subjects. . . . Eventually I got a job as a sales assistant in an electrical goods shop in Cambridge. As a matter of fact it wasn't bad, but after about a year of the same old thing every day, I realised I couldn't go on working in a shop for ever. I started looking for something with prospects. I don't know what got me thinking seriously about the RAF—I was in the ATC for a while as a kid and I went through a stage then of wanting to be a pilot, like they all do. Also, being in Cambridge, you can't ignore the RAF, they pound about the skies all the time! Anyway, the careers office said I should try for a commission, so I duly went to Biggin Hill and they turned me down. Looking back, I'm not surprised. I was so immature it wasn't true. I joined as an airman.*' As with Peter Stevens, the possibility of commissioning from the ranks has been mentioned to Simon, and he is pleased, but he has been advised to wait a year before taking the matter further.

Eight months ago, Simon married Ingrid, a girl he had known 'on and off' since sixth form days, when they studied the same 'A' levels. She went on to train and qualify as a diagnostic radiographer. At the moment, she earns more money than Simon and has a more demanding and higher-status job. They have no immediate plans to start a family, but hope to do so 'in four or five years'.

Peter, Derek and Simon have all begun their military careers in the non-commissioned ranks of their respective Services. The next three men entered the military as officers. Interestingly, there are several parallels between SAC Simon Watkins' background and that of the first officer, Lieutenant Philip Cooke RN.

Phil's parents were school teachers, and after a lot of indecision he too, decided to teach. At school he gained a provisional place at university to read Education, but a failed 'A' level set him back. His parents wanted him to re-sit the exam, but a week after the 'A' level disappointment he was taken for a joy-ride in a helicopter and was instantly 'hooked'. He wrote off to all three Services enquiring about helicopter pilot training and, as a result, applied to join the Fleet Air Arm. Now, at twenty-five years old, he is approaching the end of his original eight-year engagement and will have to decide whether or not to try and make a full career in the military. As a helicopter pilot he rates his job-satisfaction as *'very high'*—particularly as he now has a training role which he relishes—*'It's the teacher coming out in me after all!'*

Pauline, his wife, is a year younger than Phil and their families have known one another since they were children. *'Though'*, Pauline explains *'we didn't start going out together until a New Year's Eve party when I was back from college and Phil was on leave from the Navy'*. Pauline (like Simon's wife, Ingrid) left school to enter the medical world—as a physiotherapist. She and Phil were married two years ago and she worked until recently, when their baby daughter Louise was born. Their early experience of married life did not include a *'proper home'*—*'Phil lived in the Wardroom and I lived in our rented flat near to the hospital—which was two hours away. It was the best we could do, I couldn't get work any closer.'* Pauline did not seriously consider giving up her job at that stage, neither did Phil attempt to persuade her to do so. . . .

Flight Lieutenant Mike Harrison and his wife Jenny both have fathers who served in the RAF. Mike's father was a doctor, and as Mike grew up, he moved house *'countless times—all over the world.'* He and his brother went to boarding school from the age of eight and became seasoned air travellers, flying out to their parents at holiday times. From an early age he wanted to join the RAF and, for most of his boyhood, dreamed of being a fast-jet pilot. At school he was bright and was clearly destined for university; the RAF obligingly awarded him a sixth form scholarship and a university cadetship. He studied Aeronautical Engineering, still with the ultimate aim of becoming a pilot, but he did well at his subject and in the end, decided to stick to it. *'I came into the RAF as an Engineer and I haven't regretted it. I've had two super tours—one in UK, one overseas, and there's every possibility I'll get a research job or an instructing job next. What's more, I have a reasonably marketable qualification if at some point I do leave.'*

Jenny, at thirty-one, is marginally older than Mike. Her father was an NCO and, as aircrew, he flew in transport aircraft. This enabled Jenny's childhood to be quite stable, rather unmilitary. The family lived in their own house in a Wiltshire village. *'Dad was always away, but we never moved house at all. I went to one primary school, one secondary school and then to university.'* Jenny read Modern Languages and, wanting to teach adults, she joined the RAF as an Education Officer. After serving for just over three years, she met and married Mike, and after their marriage they served on the same station. Two years later, Jenny left the Service, expecting their first child. They now have two small boys, aged four and a half and two.

Army Captain Paul Lefever and Alison Macdonald are in their late twenties. They have known each other for two years and live together when they can—they each have a flat near to their own place of work. Although their relationship is stable they do not plan to marry until they judge that the time is right for them to have children. They lead semi-independent lives and feel that this arrangement works very well.

Paul's father was an Army officer but retired with the rank of Major when Paul was young. *'There was a lot of "Army influence" at home, lots of talk about Army times, but I don't remember the events, just the family reminiscences.'* Surprisingly, Paul attended a comprehensive school—'surprisingly' because he seems every inch 'ex-public school'. He dresses casually but carefully; his clothes are expensive. He speaks well and is relaxed and self-assured. He appears the model young officer and his career has been a copy-book progression from one level of responsibility to another. Attendance at the Army Staff College with promotion to Major to follow are reckoned to be in the offing.

In fact, he decided on an Army career relatively late, obtaining a good degree in History and working his way around the USA before applying to enter Sandhurst.

His partner, Alison, lives in London and is a research chemist for a large industrial concern. She is highly paid and is single-minded about her work. The couple see each other at weekends and occasionally for an evening during the week, but separations are frequent, as Paul's career constantly takes him away. Alison attends some regimental social functions as Paul's girl-friend, but he often goes alone: *'It's OK for him to do that as a bachelor; if we were married he'd be expected to bring me along to everything.'* She adds ruefully: *'I'd like one day to have Paul's children—but I find it difficult to see myself as an Army wife. . . .'*

*   *   *

Social and Educational Backgrounds

Looking at the social backgrounds of these six couples, and indeed, of the sample as a whole, the chief factor which impresses itself is that, by and large, the families from which the 'high flyers' come are not wildly different from one another. One would guess that few of the interviewees—

commissioned or non-commissioned—would feel unbearably uncomfortable in the parental homes of any of the others. Admittedly, some exceptions spring to mind. For instance, an Army Captain was interviewed who serves with a socially élite regiment and who neatly fits the stereotypical image of the 'Army Officer'. The product of an aristocratic family with a tradition of Army service, he attended a well-known public school and then entered Sandhurst. His wife is from a similar background and he supports her and their children with the aid of a useful private income. An intelligent young man with science 'A' levels, his privileged start in life is far removed from the experience of the most junior (though not the youngest) man in the sample. This man holds the rank of Private and has been in the Army for only a short time. A tough-talking Cockney, he was brought up by a series of foster-parents in south-east London. Before joining the Army he had had several jobs—and one or two brushes with the law. His quick-wittedness singles him out from the crowd and goes some way towards compensating for his lack of educational qualifications, social graces, even career ambitions. As he is bright, he will probably get on in the Army—though not far enough or fast enough to enable him to move easily into the middle classes.

Although it is possible, even in this small sample, to find an example of men from opposite ends of the social spectrum, in reality most Servicemen hail from the social mainstream of British life. And amongst 'high-flyers' in particular, it seems that the traditional polarisation between the officer/gentleman background and the other-ranks/working man background no longer holds true.

In the past, that is, before the Second World War, the military took its directly commissioned officers almost exclusively from the families of the 'ruling classes'. The traditional link between upper-class families and military service remains significant in Britain, particularly in certain elements of the Army. Some regiments still cling tenaciously to a socially élitist image amongst their officer corps—although nowadays 'breeding' alone counts for little, if not tied to a degree of ability—even in the Guards! In reality, the commissioned sector of all three Services has, since the War, been open to bright young men from a wide variety of social backgrounds. For the able, a commission in the military has long been a passport to upward social mobility; and this passport still exists, though its importance has diminished. For, although the generalisation that working-class youngsters join the ranks and upper-class youngsters join the officer corps remains true, it is a fact that in the years since 1945, both of these social classes have shrunk, whilst the middle class has grown. And the huge lower-middle and middle class nowadays furnish good recruits for both the commissioned and the non-commissioned sectors of the military.

An interesting feature of the sample of young men 'going places' is the markedly middle class origins of a good proportion of men entering the military with non-commissioned status. Without doubt, the social backgrounds of many of the most promising new entrants to the Services are becoming closer, whether they are coming in as officers or as other-ranks. A factor which does not change is the high incidence of entrants from military families of origin. In this sample (which, after all, was not a cross-section of new entrants but a look at some 'achievers') it was the case that those who were the children of officers had in all instances, entered as officers themselves. The children of other-ranks, however, had entered either the commissioned or the non-commissioned sectors, depending upon their educational qualifications and personal qualities.

Of those whose families of origin were non-military, the overwhelming majority of achievers belonged to the middle classes, as defined by the occupation of the father. The few whose fathers were in top professional jobs (Occupational Class I according to the Goldthorpe classification) roughly balanced in number those whose fathers were in manual work or were unemployed (Occupational Classes VI and VII). But by far the largest recruiting pool for able young men was the children of the middle occupational groups: middle to lower management in industry, civil servants, local government officials, school teachers, policemen, small-businessmen and technicians. It would be true to say that more commissioned entrants came from the upper end of the occupational range and more non-commissioned entrants from the lower, but a large overlap in the middle indicates that a working-class stereotype can no longer be justified as an all pervading image of the background of the private soldier, the sailor or the airman.

Educationally, the same picture emerges, with commissioned men generally holding higher academic qualifications on entry than other-ranks. The qualifications held by the 'high-flyers' interviewed ranged from one officer who entered with a PhD to, at the other end of the scale two men, who entered with the minimum requirement of five 'O' levels; and from one non-comissioned entrant with a Bachelor's Degree to several who entered without any previous qualification. But again, a significant overlap was to be found in the middle. Take, for instance, SAC Simon Watkins, who with eight 'O' levels and one 'A' level, has a similar academic background to that of Lieutenant Phil Cooke, who holds eight 'O' levels and two 'A' levels.

The point to be emphasised is that both socially and educationally, the backgrounds of many of today's achievers are broadly similar. Commissioned and non-commissioned entrants of ability are likely to originate from middle or lower-middle class families and are likely to have left full-time education with at least 'O' levels. The striking contrast between this and the situation which obtained twenty and more years ago, is the recent arrival on the military scene of significant numbers of high calibre young men entering as Ordinary Seamen, Private Soldiers and Aircraftsmen.

Career Motivation: The Self-Image of the Young Military Man

Corporal Peter Stevens: '*Soldiering is about working closely with a few other blokes. It all comes down to platoons in the end, and every single soldier has to be able to handle his job—whatever—otherwise he's a hazard to himself and everybody else. . . . Knowing you've got a vital part to play in an operation and people are depending on you to do your job right—that's the real satisfaction. That's what keeps me in the Army.*'

Lieutenant Phil Cooke: '*If I'm honest, I see myself as a first-rate helicopter pilot. First and foremost. And a Naval officer second. If that makes it sound as though the Navy isn't important to me, that isn't right; it's just that if you ask me what I am, I immediately think "helicopter pilot", then afterwards "Naval officer".*'

This part of the discussion centred on the way in which the men saw their work, their Service, their careers. Twenty or more years ago, men apparently joined the military largely because they were attracted by the idea of being *in* the Army, Navy or RAF. 'Vocationalism' is probably too strong a word, since it has overtones of the denial of self-interest which did not necessarily characterise recruits to the military. Nevertheless, the recruit in the past was clearly looking for that particular sense of corporate identity which the Services offered. Once the man was a member of an Armed Service, his chief loyalty, his chief pride was in his membership of that institution. Is it still the same? With increasing levels of specialisation in the military demanding ever greater concentration upon training for particular work, does the overriding loyalty to the Service remain strong amongst today's young 'achievers'?

In June 1985, there was an international conference at the United States Air Force Academy on the subject of 'Institutional and Occupational Trends in Military Organisation'. The conference discussed the perceived trend within the United States military towards 'occupationalism', that is, of men regarding their military service as 'a job' rather than as a way of life. Now whilst this may present no immediate threat to standards, the occupationally orientated worker brings with him the priorities of the market place. His employer, if he wishes to retain that worker and his skills, must offer rates of pay, hours of work and conditions of work that compare favourably with those available from other possible employers. In America, it seems that, in order to keep high-quality personnel, the military has had to tread this path. The result has been a worrying blurring of the distinctions between soldier and civilian—the soldier taking on the expectations of the civilian. It is worrying because active service is uncomfortable, dangerous, frightening and exhausting and training must therefore contain all these unpleasantnesses too—difficult if one is trying to retain a work force whose outlook is becoming '*Nine to Five and Home for Dinner*'.[1]

There are those in the British military world who would claim that the British Armed Forces are moving in the same direction, if more slowly, but, fortunately, this does not appear to be so. The self-image of the British military is certainly changing, moving away from 'vocationalism'—but not moving as far as occupationalism. In an interesting paper,[2] presented at the same conference, Dr Cathy Downes outlined a broad movement within the British military towards an image of *professionalism*. The concept of the 'professional', with obligations to the community above and beyond the letter of his contract is more deeply rooted in Western European than in American culture, and the British military have consciously promoted this image of themselves, aided by their traditional links with the Crown, the Church and the aristocracy. The suggestion contained in Dr Downes' paper is that British professionalism is more satisfactory as a self-image and as a public image than the market-orientated occupationalism which is worrying the Americans. This may indeed be so, but it begs questions of its own. For instance, if the young man embarking on a military career today tends to view his commitment as a professional one, will there be corresponding losses in terms of his institutional commitment?

Returning to the sample of young 'high flyers', the first point that emerges from the interviews is that they have indeed, wholeheartedly embraced the 'Join the Professionals' image promoted by the recruiting literature. This image could not be further from '*Nine to Five and Home for Dinner*', stressing as it does, the hard and often dirty work, long hours and high standards required. Recruiting material creates a certain aura of élitism and goes out of its way to imply that the reader would probably not possess the qualities necessary to become a soldier, sailor or airman.

None of the young men interviewed minded the difficulties or dangers of their work: '*That's what sets us apart from the guys in civvy street and we're proud of it*' (Petty Officer Derek Pearson). Most actually relished periods of working long hours in uncomfortable conditions: '*Arctic survival in Norway—brilliant!*' (Corporal Peter Stevens). And they accepted the concept of discipline—both enforced and self-imposed—as an important and necessary feature of military life: '*It's good. You know where you stand; you know what's got to be done and because there's discipline, you know you can absolutely rely on everyone else*' (Senior Aircraftsman Simon Watkins).

They are not 'soft' physically and certainly not 'soft' mentally. Above all, they take enormous pride in the skills which they possess and in being able to exercise them in the most trying of conditions. Here there is a difference between the traditional and the new 'achiever'. Today's man has much more to learn, the equipment he handles is much more complex, more expensive, more deadly. Mistakes cannot be overlooked and the incompetent operator cannot be 'carried' for long. It is not surprising, therefore, that the military stresses the high standards of competence which it requires of its men. In consequence, training now leaves less time than used to be allocated for the inculcation of the traditional military ethos of *service* (in the real sense) to God, Queen and Country, and, taking its young entrants, it concentrates more on impressing upon them a conscientious spirit of professionalism—pride in one's skill, and a sense of duty to use it wisely.

In this sense, the British career military man has found himself a new image—no longer that of service as a *servant* but of service as an expert, placing his expertise at society's disposal. The sophisticated way in which the military has handled politically delicate operations in the recent past (for example, the policing role in Northern Ireland, the Iranian Embassy siege, the disarming of opposing factions in Zimbabwe, the air-drops of food to Ethiopia) has re-inforced this image both in the eyes of the general public and for the military man himself.

So far, no losses. The professional image seems a dynamic, modern and highly satisfactory one. But losses of a kind, there are, and these have to be faced.

The first is that the professional man, through his particular skills, has links with those outside the military who practice the same skills. If he is an engineer, or a computer specialist, or a personnel manager, the chances are high that he will belong to a recognised professional body and that he will want to keep abreast of developments in his own field. This consequently loosens the ties which traditionally bound the military man exclusively to his Service. Whereas in the past, the Sandhurst cadet or the RAF Swinderby boy-entrant felt he was being trained *by* the military, *for* the military, nowadays the young man tends to look upon his military training as a valuable contribution to his overall personal education—begun before joining, and with the possibility of continuation elsewhere, after leaving.

Flight Lieutant Mike Harrison: '*I came into the RAF as a well-qualified Engineer; I've been given a specialist training and some sound experience, but I could equally well work in industry or even as an academic. As it happens, I don't have any plans to leave the RAF, but I do take a professional journal and I do keep half an eye on the "Sits Vac" columns—as much as anything to see how I rate beside my civilian colleagues.*'

Petty Officer Derek Pearson: '*I'm a trained diver. I could earn good money on the rigs. I don't fancy the way of life as much—I suit the Navy and the Navy suits me—but I'm aware of the possibilities—I'd be a fool if I wasn't!*'

A second kind of loss of institutional commitment resulting from concentration on professional skills, shows itself in a lessening of willingness to devote much time or effort to activities which fall outside the professional sphere. These include secondary duties, non-specialist tasks and some social responsibilities. Of course, not all young men find all these things irksome, but most consider at least some of them to be unnecessary, degrading, sometimes infuriating. Senior Aircraftsman Simon Watkins: '*As an SAC in the General Office I get 'Joe-ed' for all sorts of odd jobs. Last week I was in the middle of collating a great pile of papers coming off the copier, when I had to stop everything and go and shove slips of paper through the letter boxes of married quarters about works services or something. . . . How can you take trouble over your work when they do things like that to you?'*

In the same vein, Corporal Peter Stevens: '*I got put into a Royal Tournament display team once. . . . There I was, poncing about like a right wally. It's got nothing to do with being a soldier. Nothing. I'd have walked out there and then if I could have.*'

And Captain Paul Lefever: '*We have an awful lot of social functions to attend. We're a very social regiment. Usually it's good fun, but there are times when your liver or your pocket says "enough", and the compulsion to attend a dinner or a cocktail party—or a ball—does rankle, and you think "Why the Hell should I? Is it really necessary for the defence of the United Kingdom?"*'

The 'old school' would reply that these things are part of the wider role of the Serviceman and should be performed with as much diligence as a man's primary task. . . .

A final difference of outlook between today's 'professional' and his traditional counterpart, is to be found in the modern man's relative lack of enthusiasm for the paternalistic way in which he might expect the military to 'look after' his family. In Britain, in the 1980s, he is not dependent on the military to house his family, educate his children and provide them with medical care; they have their own rights within the Welfare State. The notion that a military man's family should hold unswerving allegiance to his Service is therefore foreign to many newcomers—especially those with no family tradition of military service. Moreover, a significant number of the women have no desire whatever to be 'looked after' by the military. One such woman is Alison Macdonald, Capt. Paul Lefever's partner: '*I've had a chance to look at the system from the outside, as Paul's girl-friend and frankly, I don't want to get too involved—certainly not unless we decide to have children. . . . You see, you can't have a career and be an Army wife. If the Army builds quarters, you're expected to live in them, if they post your husband to Outer Mongolia, you're expected to go along, if they invite wives to an 'Open Day', you'd better be there or there'll be questions asked. It's just too difficult. The Army believes that wives are a kind of lower order of soldier with special duties of their own, and perhaps they are—but not me. Truthfully, Paul is much better off being a bachelor than having an "uncommitted" wife.*'

In the transition of the British military man's career motivation from a 'vocational' outlook to a professional one, there have been gains and there have been losses. Overall, it seems an exciting move with a great deal of potential to be tapped. Always provided the Military Establishment concentrates on building on the strengths of the emergent professional image and not on bemoaning the loss of narrower horizons and tighter institutional loyalty. Today's young achievers may have different priorities from their predecessors, but the values are still there. Captain Paul Lefever: '*In the old days someone in my position would have been, above all, a gentleman— if he wasn't, he couldn't have been an officer. As an officer his life would have been his Regiment, and promotion would have depended as much upon his ability to play polo or be entertaining at dinner as anything else. The task, the fighting task, was simply another component of the whole. . . . For me, the situation is reversed. I concentrate very hard on mastering the military task in hand—the equipment, the tactics, the manpower and so forth—and my priority in the Army is to do that well. I feel a strong emotional attachment to my Regiment, but it doesn't constitute my whole world—professional or social. As for being an officer and a gentleman, these are such nebulous concepts nowadays. . . . means having good manners I think. But you see what I mean? The value system is still there—its just been turned on its head . . .'*

*   *   *

Working Wives

The attitude of the young women in the sample towards their working after marriage was straightforward. All expected to continue in employment (or had continued) until they started a family and most expected to resume working at some point after having children. None of the husbands disagreed with this position.

This outlook is a vast change from that prevailing twenty years ago. A forty-four-year-old RAF officer's wife remembers: '*When we were first married it was almost unheard of for wives to work. On the officer's patch* [more than 150 houses] *only four of us worked, and we were looked on as* very *odd.*'

Today, not everyone who would like to work can get a job, but it is most unusual for a young woman to give up all thoughts of job or career on getting married. Certainly none of the female partners of the young men 'going places' had given up such thoughts.

Ingrid Watkins, radiographer (Senior Aircraftsman's Simon Watkins wife): '*I made up my mind to work in the medical field when I was about fourteen. Radiography was mentioned during a careers interview at school and I began working towards it from 'O' levels. . . . I love it . . . I wouldn't think of giving up to start a family yet—Simon's still at the beginning of his career, and we have to wait and see what develops. He'll get his Corporal's tapes anyway, but it would be quite nice if he went for commissioning. . . . Eventually, yes, we'd like children, then I'd definitely stop the full-time bit. Hopefully though, I'd be able to do some locum work—to keep my hand in.*' Ingrid, like most of the professionally qualified wives, considers her training a basis for employment (though not necessarily full-time employment) throughout her working life. To date, she has not given any serious thought to the possibility of her not being *able* to work should she accompany her husband on an overseas tour or to a remote base in the United Kingdom. It is a problem she may well have to face in the future, and because of her clear expectation of a career in radiography, it will be a very difficult problem to face.

Pauline Cooke, physiotherapist (Lieutenant Phil Cooke's wife) has already had to make decisions about military life, family and career: *'I've stopped work completely. While Phil's based here there's no hope of part-time or anything. Not that I mind at the moment. Louise* [six months] *is quite a handful—it takes all my energy just looking after her! We'd like to have another baby soon, so I think I'll be out of the labour-market for at least five or six years. But I do miss it. I miss the company and the satisfaction of doing something you know you're good at. And its weird not having your own money—it makes you feel like a "kept woman". One thing I have done is to get involved with teaching swimming on a voluntary basis, its the nearest I can get to filling the gap.'*

Karen Stevens, bank clerk (Corporal Peter Steven's wife) has also given up her job now that she has a baby: *'At first it was a real treat, not having to be up and out at the crack of dawn in all weathers—but it wore off ever so quickly. Don't get me wrong, I wouldn't change having Alexander for the world—he's tremendous—what I'd really like is a little job where I could take him along in his playpen. Even cleaning perhaps. I'm not bored—I've got some good friends around here, but I'd like to have just a little bit of money to call my own again. To be able to buy the odd thing without having to be sensible* all *the time because I'm not earning.'*

Jenny Harrison, education officer (Flight Lieutenant Mike Harrison's wife) has been out of full-time work for five years, but: *'I've been extremely lucky; from time to time I've taken classes on camp—French and German mainly, but I also teach Russian. This is the second tour where I've managed to carry on in a small way, and it's ideal. I can fit in preparation and marking around the children, and I pay a neighbour to look after them when Mike can't do it. I hope it lasts, but I can't rely on it.'* Jenny's husband Mike was not alone amongst husbands in the sample in expressing a sense of guilt about the uncertainties of his wife's future: *'Jenny had a career in her own right that was every bit as promising as mine. OK, she gave it up, and that was her decision, but my job and the fact that it can take us anywhere at a moment's notice, effectively prevents her from planning ahead at all. I mean, casual jobs are fine while the children are little, but she's not what you'd call "highly domesticated", so when the boys go to school she'll be looking around for something more substantial. How we play things from then on I'm not sure. . . .'*

Lesley Pearson, secretary (Petty Officer Derek Pearson's wife) is less troubled. She left school with two 'O' levels, a bundle of CSEs, spectacularly good looks and a sunny personality: *'I take life as it comes. . . . I had a terrific time in the Wrens and I was sorry to leave, but we've made the move and I'm pleased now. . . . The secretarial course I took was hard, but it was a good training and I've never been out of work except when I didn't want to work. I'm looking forward to the baby. Derek and I want lots of children—well three or four at any rate—we're both from big families ourselves. I expect, in the very long run, I shall probably go out to work again, but not till the youngest child's about ten or eleven. I think children need a mum at home—mine always was. When I do go back, it might be secretarial work or it might be anything—whatever turns up.'*

Even Lesley, with the nearest approach to a 'traditional' female viewpoint, puts great stress on getting a sound training for work. She has enjoyed life, both in the Wrens and more recently as a secretary and certainly did not see these occupations as mere time-fillers until marriage and babies came on the scene. She envisages a wholehearted commitment to domesticity for the immediate future, but even Lesley does not picture herself as a full-time housewife for the rest of her active life.

Households

This part of the discussion featured the domestic side of the lives of the young couples in the sample. Where do they live? How do they live? What do they understand by the term 'home'?

Any discussion about housing and households must begin with the acknowledgement that a house is more than just a shelter, and a neighbourhood more than just a collection of shelters. A house is a territorial space, affording privacy from the outside world and proclaiming to it—through its appearance—something about the character of its inhabitants. A neighbourhood too, presents an image to anyone coming in to live, work or trade, and satisfaction (or the lack of it) with that image is very important to the individuals who make up the community. So, how did these couples view 'home'?

Some of the young people still thought of 'home' as their parental home. This was noticeable amongst couples who did not have children, and amongst couples where both partners came from the same or nearby home-towns. They tended to think of their own household as an offshoot from the more stable, enduring 'home' from which they had originated. Karen Stevens: *'When I say "We're going home" I mean, up North, to our parents' home. I talk about our married quarter as home too, but not in the same way. It's hard to explain . . . home is where your roots are—your proper roots—not just where you happen to be at the moment.'*

Couples with children, and those where husband and wife came from different parts of the country, and those from mobile military families more readily defined their own households as 'home'.

All the couples were preoccupied with home-making (in the sense of creating and defining their own, distinctive 'territorial space') to some degree. Most, being relatively newly married, were in the habit of spending a portion of their income on acquisitions for their home. Generally, the men in the sample were highly involved in the home-making process; most purchases of durable goods were likely to be made by husbands and wives together.

In common with the '*Social Trends (1985)*' findings for the population at large, young military couples share household management tasks to a greater extent than did their counterparts twenty years ago. As would be expected, men whose partners were in full-time employment took a much greater part in running their homes—cooking, shopping and cleaning being tasks which were frequently shared in the case of almost all these couples. Ingrid Watkins: '*Simon and I do our weekly shopping together on a Friday evening and if we run out of anything during the week, either of us might get it—whoever remembers. The evening meal is started by the person who arrives home first—and I have to say that it's usually Simon during the week, so I do more of the cooking at the weekend. We both wash up, we both clean, we both use the washing machine; I do more of the ironing. Simon does most of the 'handyman' stuff, but I'm quite good at fiddling with electrical gadgets. Simon also pays the bills and keeps track of our joint account, because he's better at it than I am.*'

There was a noticeable emphasis amongst all the couples on sharing tasks according to aptitude rather than along traditional male/female lines. Many of the women, for instance, managed the family's money and paid all the bills, both because they were efficient at the task and because for some, the frequent absences of their husbands made it a more practicable arrangement.

Where families included children, a more traditional bias was in evidence, with wives undertaking a much greater proportion of the housework than their husbands. Even so, most husbands were accustomed to helping with cooking, shopping and cleaning tasks, and most wives helped with some maintenance and repair jobs—especially decorating. All of which makes the point that the belief that young husbands nowadays take a more active part in the day-to-day running of their households than did their fathers, is true, and that young military men are no exception.

Choosing to set up home in a married quarter, or deciding against this course of action has become an issue for discussion by today's young couples. A majority will prefer to live in quarters, but this is no longer an automatic or a career-long preference. For years past, the object of the married military man was to be accompanied by his wife and children whenever possible, and to this end, great pressure was put upon the Ministry of Defence to build more married quarters. Until quite recently, a young married man would have had to wait—perhaps a long time—to be allocated a quarter on posting, and his dream was to be able to move from post to post knowing that accommodation for his family would always be rapidly provided. At that time, of course, house prices were lower, and a man's gratuity at the end of his service would allow him to enter the market. Now, almost all the couples interviewed said either that they owned, or that at some point they hoped to buy, their own home. A majority of these also expressed a wish to live in their property rather than let it to tenants as an investment during their military service.

Two factors seem to be at work here. The most obvious is the financial factor, in that it makes economic sense for people who can afford mortgage repayments to buy rather than rent property. The other factor is more subtle and more contentious; it is that the 'pull' of the military community is not as strong now as it was in the past. One reason for this may be that the Services do not receive so many of their entrants at such a young and impressionable age as once they did. Twenty years ago, a large majority of recruits joined the Armed Forces more or less straight from school, certainly straight from home. Today, a larger proportion—especially amongst the officer corps—have been away to college or have had some experience of flat-sharing and looking after themselves before they come into the military. Even if they haven't, it is a common enough experience amongst the young for most to identify with the idea of domestic independence before marriage. Once in the Services, those who have been independent find it harder to adjust to barrack-style communal living for protracted lengths of time and lead the way towards finding non-Service accommodation slightly away from the military community in order to regain a measure of that domestic independence. Some senior officers find this trend quite worrying. A Lieutenant Colonel: '*Young officers, straight from training; they've hardly been in the Army five minutes before they're asking permission to live out. I insist that they stay for at least a year in the Officers' Mess, otherwise we'll end up with a generation of officers who neither know nor care about the Army way of doing things.*'

When the young men marry, most will take advantage of the availability of married quarters, but few look upon life in married quarters as part of their *commitment* to the military. The six couples whose descriptions and comments have been highlighted, are fairly representative of the sample in general. Three of the couples live in married quarters, two in their own homes and one rents private-sector accommodation.

Captain Paul Lefever is very used to looking after himself (since leaving home to go to university he has spent only two years in a hall of residence and intermittant spells in Army messes, where his domestic arrangements were taken care of). At present he shares the rental of a spacious house with another Army bachelor. Alison, his partner, rents a London flat which serves as the couple's social base.

Lieutenant Phil Cooke and his wife Pauline have not lived in married quarters yet, and have no plans to do so. They have bought a tiny, two bedroomed cottage in the country, about ten miles away from Phil's base. Several Naval families live in the same village—indeed, one of the biggest and most attractive houses there is owned by a retired Chief Petty Officer—

but the Navy is only one small element of what is predominantly a farming population. When Phil is posted, he and Pauline intend to sell the cottage and buy another house near their new base. Although they would be entitled to rent a larger and better equipped married quarter than they could afford to buy, they are not tempted to do this. Phil: *'We like our own house. It's not just the investment . . . it's good to get home at the end of the day and come into a different world—right away from the Navy.'*

Flight Lieutenant Mike Harrison and Jenny, on the other hand, have lived in quarters since their marriage. But both had a taste of bed-sit living during university days and both lived out of the Officers' Mess for periods of time when they were single. Jenny: *'We've enjoyed being in quarters enormously—probably we're the right sort. By that I mean we're both outgoing, gregarious . . . we make friends quickly and get involved in the social life. We haven't any plans to buy a house at the moment, but we talk about it incessantly; it's definitely "on the agenda".'* Mike, when asked whether he thought that moving out of quarters would in some way be 'turning his back' on the military community, replied, *'We wouldn't be rejecting "patch life" because we would move back into quarters if I was posted somewhere which was inaccessible from the house. We like quarters, but it would be nice to own our own home and to have the occasional slice of normal, civilian-style living.'*

There are, too, some senior officers who view the desire of young people to live 'out' in the local community as, on balance, beneficial to the military. A Major: *'These youngsters are superb ambassadors for the Army in the area. They get to know all sorts of local people and they can represent the point of view of the Service better than any amount of official "community relations". I think it's a healthy trend, myself.'*

Petty Officer Derek Pearson and his wife Lesley lived briefly in a Portsmouth married quarter before moving into a small, modern terraced house in a nearby town. Both sets of parents helped with the deposit and they are now proud property owners. Lesley: *'We might have waited a bit longer, but we didn't like the quarter we were in. I thought it would be a help, leaving the Wrens, to sort-of stay with the Navy for a while—but it wasn't. The house was in rotten condition and the neighbours weren't particularly friendly. And it was just an estate. It didn't feel "Navy" to me. . . . So we bought.'*

In contrast, Corporal Peter Stevens and his wife Karen have lived in quarters since their marriage, and are happy to continue this way for the forseeable future. Peter: *'To begin with, we can't afford a decent house down here* [South of England]. *We could buy one in Yorkshire, near our parents and let it, but it'd be a burden more than an asset . . . I think for as long as you're in the Army you're better off saving with one of the schemes and living in quarters where the Army sends you.'*

Senior Aircraftsman Simon Watkins and Ingrid have just moved out of a flat and into a married quarter. It is situated on a large, rather bleak-looking estate, but inside, the house is smart. Some stylish furnishings and pictures proclaim the distinctive tastes of the young tenants. They are pleased with the move, but unsure about the question of living in quarters for the duration of Simon's career. *'We haven't thought that far ahead and until I know which way my career's going to go, I don't think we can. . . .'* And Ingrid: *'I'm quite content to be in quarters for the time being—but eventually I'd like a place of our own.'*

*   *   *

Parenting

The final part of the discussion focussed on issues of parenting. Some of the couples interviewed already had children—though all were under school age—and some were hoping to start a family in the future.

Attitudes of the sample towards the task of parenting show clearly the extent to which young married couples today have moved towards the idea of symmetry in marital responsibilities. The notion that fathers should regularly take care of their infants and small children was accepted, absolutely and without qualification, by all the couples interviewed. Those men who had children were all involved in their day-to-day care (whenever they were at home) and all expressed great satisfaction in the role of fatherhood.

Phil Cooke: *'I was present at Louise's birth and I held her when she was— oh, about two minutes old. She's a smashing kid. Except for breast-feeding I've been able to do everything for her—nappy changing, the lot. . . . When I come in from work on a normal day I bath her and play with her while Pauline gets dinner. To be honest, I'm slightly dreading going back to sea. I know I shall miss so many little things in her development—time that can't be replaced.'*

Mike Harrison's elder son is due to begin primary schooling in the near future: *'It's a very big step for him, he doesn't settle to new things easily and we want his first experiences of 'real' school to be positive ones. Yesterday, Jenny and I went to an afternoon session at the school to meet his teacher and so on. . . . No, I certainly didn't feel embarrassed about taking the afternoon off work—if there'd been an exercise or an extra-heavy work-load I wouldn't have gone—but under normal circumstances, my son's education comes higher on my list of priorities than routine work.'*

Such paternal concern for the everyday welfare of their children is a relatively new component in the image of the military father. It certainly seems more pronounced amongst the 'high flyers' than amongst the 'plodders' of the military world. Conversations with wives (of the kind to be found in later chapters) indicate that there are still many men who like to stay close to their fellows, be 'one of the lads' and accept little responsibility for the running of their home or the upbringing of their children. They were, however, not to be found in the sample of 'achievers'. Here, the macho ideology that birth and babies are women's matters and that dedication to one's comrades and one's Service must take precedence over family commitments is waning. Young fathers, inside as well as outside the military, *expect* to be involved in the care of their children. A Fleet Air Arm Squadron Commander's wife related that a young officer had recently told her husband he would not be able to fly on a particular routine mission, as it was his daugher's birthday. She remarked: '*He was given pretty short shrift I'm told; but I rather admired him. A few years ago, if it had even crossed a fellow's mind that he'd prefer not to fly on his daughter's birthday, he would* never *have said so, for fear his mates would ridicule him. Things* are *different now.*'

But if attitudes towards the role of fatherhood have changed, military commitments which take fathers away from home have not. The resentment which many fathers feel in missing continuous contact with their children often surprises them. The young military father, like any other, has absorbed the ideal of 'involved fatherhood' and then seems to be frustrated at every turn when he tries to put this ideal into practice. Peter Stevens: '*I knew in my job I'd be away from home a lot, and that when I was away Karen would have to bring up Alexander on her own. But knowing that didn't actually stop me from getting up-tight about it. . . . When Alexander was only a few weeks old, we went to Northern Ireland for four months. When we left I felt terrible—like I'd deserted Karen . . . Having a new baby is a responsibility, and there I was, miles away, no help at all. . . . But then you adjust to it and you feel guilty for not missing home as much as you think you ought to—but if you didn't adjust and went round moping all the time, you'd be no bloody good anyway.*' Karen interjected. '*My mum came down for a couple of weeks, and the neighbours were very good, but basically, I had to get on with it and cope. There were plenty of times when I did feel deserted.*' Peter continued: '*Coming home after four months, Alexander was unrecognisable. I mean, I'd had photos and stuff, but I wasn't prepared for* such *a change . . . It took weeks before he felt like he really was my son . . . I don't know if you ever get used to it, this part-time father business, but its the one thing about Army life that sometimes makes me bitter.*'

The couples in the sample were asked whether they had thought about the effect which a military way of life would have on their children's education. The expectation was that few of the young parents and probably none of the couples yet to produce children would have given much time to considering this distant question. But this assumption was quite mistaken. *All* of the parents and most of the prospective parents had already begun to think about the thorny subject of education.

Derek Pearson: '*Getting a decent set of paper qualifications is* so *important today, you can't afford to muck about with your kids' education. They can't be changing schools too often, especially as they get older, otherwise they never know where they are with the work and the teachers and their friends. That's one of the main reasons we've decided on a settled home from the start. Boarding school? No, not for us.'*

The boarding school option (the Ministry of Defence gives Servicemen who desire it an allowance towards the cost of a boarding education to give children continuity and stability at school, no matter where parents postings may take them) was something that had been widely discussed, but a large majority at this stage of their lives were not keen on the idea. Paul Lefever—who as yet, has no children: *'I'm not happy about sending children to boarding school. Army life is very hard on children, but, frankly, I don't think boarding school is the answer. I suppose, at the crucial points of 'O' and 'A' levels, you have to settle your wife and children and accept that if the Army requires you to be elsewhere, you must go without them.'*

Of 'the six couples' only one individual—Mike Harrison—is firmly in favour of sending his sons to boarding school. Jenny, his wife, is ambivalent: *'I'm not pro-boarding school at all—but you have to be realistic. Children don't like change, well ours don't, and I don't think its fair to make them continually re-adjust—after all,* they *didn't choose the life, we did. So for this reason I'm prepared to consider sending the boys away to school—but not at eight, like Mike—it would have to be at eleven.'*

Pauline Cooke is also being realistic: *'Phil and I say "no" to boarding school now. I can't imagine ever parting with Louise. But that's now. We may feel different when the time comes. I've got a friend who thought like I do, but then they got posted into the catchment area of a really dreadful school. They had no choice, the only other school in the area—not surprisingly—was full. Her children had an absolutely miserable year before they finally went off to board. . . . You see, the trouble is, if you decide to keep them with you, you have so little choice about the schools they have to go to.'*

Peter Stevens: *'Put it this way; if I come out of the Army it'll be because of the hassle it causes for the family. I love soldiering, but I hate not seeing my son for months on end, and I worry about how he'll cope at school with all the moving. If I stay in, I reckon we'll have to think very carefully about boarding. Not that we like the idea . . . but it would have to be thought about.'*

The young men in the sample clearly take the pleasures and responsibilities of fatherhood very seriously. The chief difference between their attitude and that of their predecessors seems to be one of expectation. Twenty and more years ago, young military men normally accepted that public duty came first, and that their wives would inevitably shoulder the main burden of bringing up their children. Nowadays, this assumption is not made. On the contrary, young men expect to play an active part in the care and socialisation of their children and there are signs that they feel quite resentful when reality falls short of expectation. How these men will come to terms with the more limited, more traditional role of fatherhood which is consistant with the realities of military life, time will tell.

*   *   *

The young couples who took part in the interviews had much in common. In stressing similarities of background and outlook, huge differences that remain between some individuals have not been dwelt upon because they are atypical of the group as a whole. However, as mentioned earlier, young officers from well-heeled upper middle class families, with Oxford accents, old school ties and immense self-confidence are still there, amongst the 'achievers', as are bright young men in the ranks, from traditional working-class families. They are a diverse group, but it is argued that the social and educational distance between the highest and the lowest calibre of entrant is not as wide as it used to be, and that a new gap—a generation gap—is emerging. Today's young military man, particularly the more able and articulate man, does have different attitudes and aspirations from those of career Servicemen in times past.

How will these young men and their families fit in to the social mould which the military cast for itself generations ago? In order to consider this question, one must look at the life of military communities now, the ways in which these communities are changing, and the plight of individuals who cannot find personal stability in this close society, caught up in inevitable social change.

*   *   *

CHAPTER 3

Military Communities: 'The Married Patch'

Married Quarters—Why They Exist

Used in the singular, the phrase 'the military community' normally means the men of the Armed Services. However, its plural, 'military communities' as used here, refers to neighbourhoods inhabited by members of the military with their families. For the most part, these are estates of married quarters—commonly known as 'married patches'—built in close proximity to the military bases.

There seem to be two important reasons for the existence of married quarters; the first is practical and related to goals of military efficiency, the second is (at least partly) humanitarian. As discussed in Chapter 1, married accommodation was first provided by the Army and was associated with a desire to eradicate the hoardes of camp followers and give aid and status to the recognised dependants of the soldier. It also provided semi-permanent accommodation for the married military man close to his place of duty. Since the *raison d'être* of a military force is to respond as quickly as possible to a threat from an enemy, it is desirable that the Serviceman should be able to reach his place of work within a short time of leaving his home. There was thus a sound military reason for the establishment of married quarter estates on or near bases. The policy worked well, and a pleasing consequnce was the extension of feelings of loyalty to the Regiment and the Army from the soldier's wife and children. Married accommodation became an important ingredient in the move to acquire a highly committed soldier, who, with his family, would be respectable, grateful and loyal. Over the years, military housing estates have developed into distinctive communities, and, as in any community, members had—and still have—to conform to certain standards of conduct and opinion in order to remain acceptable to the group. A gentle but steady pressure on hearts and minds is therefore exerted by the married patch community over its members; families help each other to cope with the vicissitudes of military life and learn to live within the rules—written and unwritten—of the Service. The cost to the Ministry of Defence of maintaining base housing is immense, but the reasons for its existence remain.

It has already been established that the spending of money on rented accommodation when a man's income could support a mortgage on a home of his own, does not make good sense. However, many Service personnel feel that the benefits derived from living in quarters are great, the worry small, and are happy to take the housing that is offered. A further number buy themselves a house, not to live in, but as an investment, to get into the property market. A tenant is found for the house, or sometimes an elderly parent is accommodated there—giving the Serviceman a house at the end of his career and the parent a little less financial worry.

Asking couples who choose to live in quarters, why they do so, the commonest replies revolve around four factors: cost, convenience, career and community-spirit.

Cost

For many young Servicemen, a mortgage is not an option; they do not earn enough to buy a house. The numbers of junior married men whose earnings place them below the official poverty line fluctuate. At the time of writing, the numbers entitled to Family Income Supplement (FIS) are relatively low, but in years when military pay has fallen behind that of other groups (as during the mid-1970s) numbers on FIS have risen and have probably included a number of young married officers with children.

Those for whom a mortgage is out of the question, and those who are waiting to buy a house—when they know the location of the next posting, or whether promotion will be forthcoming, or after the baby is born— cannot usually find a better standard of rented accommodation for a similar price in the private sector. The houses may not be beautiful, but there is no doubt that most are solid, well maintained and contain all the essential facilities for a reasonable standard of living. In fact, when military bases are situated in rural areas, as are many Army and RAF stations, Servicemen are hard-pressed to find any private rented accommodation at all.

Convenience

'We didn't get married to live apart.' 'He hasn't spent all that time at sea for us to be apart the first time he has a shore job.' 'Separations are part and parcel of the life, but if you live in quarters you can make the best of the time you do *have together.'* Some typical remarks of Service wives, concerned to keep families together as much as possible. Living close to his work-place enables a man to spend a greater part of his off-duty time with his family, and again, it is frequently the case that around the more remote military bases there *is* no other housing apart from married quarters. So if a man wishes to have his family with him, it is married quarters or nothing.

Career

This is a factor which only really applies to senior officers, and even then, it appears, only to the Army and the RAF. Within the Army and the RAF, there are certain command appointments with which a married man will receive a military house *ex officio*—with the job. He is obliged to move his family there and pay the rent, otherwise, in many cases, he does not get the job. This policy is based on the regimental tradition of the unit as an extended family, with the Commanding Officer and his wife as Patriarch and Matriarch. Today, when some military bases employ thousands of men and women, the CO and his wife haven't a hope of knowing even a tenth of them, but their role is symbolic. Off base, attending local functions, they represent the comfortable face of the military to the rest of the community, and on the base, they provide a model of 'military marriage' for younger and more junior people. The Navy seem to manage without getting too hot under the collar about how this role is performed, by whom, and with what degree of efficiency. It took centuries before they recognised that sailors had families at all, and they remain the least paternalistic about family welfare—and the most open-minded about how it can best be achieved. Having said this, it is generally assumed that a married Naval officer in command of a shore base will move his wife into 'the residence' and that she will undertake a certain number of official duties—unpaid, of course. Unlike the RAF and most sections of the Army, however, he is unlikely to be passed over for a second, third or even fourth choice candidate (as *has* happened in the case of RAF command appointments) if he declines to take his wife.

Community Spirit

In the course of this investigation, one of the topics discussed with military wives of some years standing, was 'favourite postings': postings they look back upon with particular fondness. It was noticeable how many times a tour of duty was mentioned when the couple were quite newly married, had young children and were living on a married quarters estate. At this age and stage of life, the military community can and does provide support and companionship from the many young families 'in the same boat'. An RSM's wife remembers: '*None of us had our mums, we didn't know that much about babies but we did have each other. We were in and out of each other's houses all the time . . . what do you do about nappy rash? . . . is he teething do you think? . . . should I take him to the doctor? We got through somehow—and we didn't half have a laugh.*'

Support was also available when the men went away. A Wing Commander's wife: '*Our husbands were Flight Lieutenants in those days, and when the Squadron went off on detachment, we just rallied round. I often used to change plugs and mend fuses for people I remember, and I had a neighbour who would always look after my children if I needed to go shopping or anything. ... They were good times. ...'*

This kind of supportiveness is not a thing of the past; it is to be found on all married patches and it is most in evidence in times of adversity. Bereavement through active service (*386* soldiers have died in Ulster alone since the 'Troubles' began) or through accidents (the military handles dangerous equipment day after day, and occasionally, accidents happen) is by no means an everyday occurrence, but after even a short involvement with the military, most people will know, or know of, someone who has lost his life. In such cases the community will close ranks, and a wife living in quarters will usually be treated by her neighbours not with pity, but with feelings of solidarity and shared loss. *'There, but for the grace of God, go I.'* Everyone knows that Service life is not a safe option. There will usually be a friend or neighbour around who has seen sudden bereavement before; there are, too, the customary visits from those less close which tangibly express community concern—the Padre will call, the doctor will call, the 'Boss' will and and so, probably, will his wife. It makes grief no easier to bear, but it does *allow* it.

A Naval NCO's wife whose husband died recently said: *'It was terrible ... but through the Wives' Club I already knew two Navy widows and they were a great help to me. ... Like them, I decided not to move out of the area but to keep as many links here as possible. ... I've bought a house in town but I've still got lots of friends in quarters. I'll always feel part of the Navy, and actually, it's more important to me now—to feel Navy—than it was when my husband was alive.'*

There is also the way in which 'the system' takes over when an emergency hits a military community. A senior officer: *'When the Belize affair blew up, we had only hours notice we were going in. The last our wives saw of us was the TV newsreel of us boarding the aircraft at Brize Norton; they had no idea how long we'd be away, whether we'd have to fight—nothing. But when we'd gone, no-one had to* tell *my wife she was the 'contact-person', she* knew. *As the CO's wife she was the one who got in touch with everybody, she made sure news was passed on and she went back to the authorities if there were problems. It was her job. ...'*

The Falklands War showed something of the strength of the wives of the military community under pressure. At RNAS Culdrose, the Navy kept the Wives' Club building constantly open and supplied tea and coffee. This provided a meeting place, a focal point both for wives in quarters and those living in the surrounding area, and the women sustained one another. They kept in touch by telephone, by meetings and visits, and the wives of the senior officers kept closely in touch with the base. Even so, they, like everyone else, learned what was happening from their radios and tele-visions—which were almost permanently switched on. One wife said: *'At one point the children and I went up to stay with my husband's parents. They were desperately worried and they very much wanted us to be with them—but after a few days I knew we couldn't stay. We had to come back.'* For these women it was a nightmarish situation, but one in which they really were able to draw strength from one another.

*   *   *

Peculiarities of the Military Housing System

As we have seen, the availability of military housing is considered very helpful by a majority of young married couples. It takes the anxiety out of finding a first home which is financially within reach, near to the husband's work place and providing a reasonable standard of comfort. Though rents are not particularly low, they are not high either and furthermore, they are standardised, so that a house in suburban London is no more expensive to rent than one in, say, rural Wales. Military housing is particularly valued by young people with small children, and, it seems, by quite a number of older couples who have no children. Here, where the bond between husband and wife is uncomplicated by consideration for the needs of other dependants, it is especially important for the two to be able to remain together if they wish to, despite postings to out-of-the-way places or changes of job at unexpected times. Although most couples will, at some point, think about buying a house of their own, the availability of married quarters does give them flexibility in their approach to the property market, secure in the knowledge that come what may, they will have a roof over their heads.

However, with security comes lack of choice. A family renting a house in the private sector is limited only by what they can afford in the area in which they want to live. Within that area they may feel it important to settle in a particular locality, or, equally, to avoid certain neighbourhoods and be prepared to pay for the privilege. They may want a large house with a garden, or a compact modern flat, or a cottage in the country. They may be chiefly concerned with economy and be seeking the cheapest possible accommodation, being resigned to putting up with the discomforts which this might entail. A military tenant finds he has to take more or less what he is given. Geographically, he is generally obliged to rent a house which is administered by the unit at which he is stationed. Thus, he cannot for instance, decide to rent an empty house at a base in Buckinghamshire— perhaps because his wife's mother lives nearby, or he likes the local schools—while he commutes to London, or Salisbury or Gloucester. Moreover, he cannot choose to pay over the odds in order to rent a particularly desirable house, or to opt for the smallest, most humble dwelling in order to save money. Military houses are allocated, and allocated basically according to rank. The higher the rank of the tenant, the 'posher' the house. Most Commanding Officers of military bases occupy very posh houses indeed; imposing residences with house-staff and gardener, big enough to accommodate a large family comfortably. It is a shame that by the time they reach such exalted heights, their children are usually grown up, and the top man and his wife rattle around 'The House' planning official dinner parties and worrying about the rent and about the mortgage and maintenance of their own home—probably miles away. The junior soldier, sailor or airman on the other hand, will qualify only for the most basic of available housing. If he has no children, one child or two young children of the same sex, he will be entitled to a modest two bedroomed house or flat with a small kitchen and bathroom and a single living room with sitting and dining areas, furnished, if he wishes; rent to be deducted from pay at source. It will be adequate for his needs, but he cannot, for example, say that his wife is earning good money and that they would like to rent one of the larger houses, perhaps on the officers' estate, where they could keep a bedroom spare for visitors and barbecue in privacy on the lawn. The very idea!

Officers' and other-ranks' accommodation is strictly separate, and even when it is contained within one estate, the dividing line is abundantly clear. Housing, like everything else in the military, is linked to rank and seniority. Need comes second to this, with numbers of children being taken into consideration in the allocation of two, three or four bedroomed dwellings. When the demand for quarters exceeds supply, a waiting list operates, and a man's position on the list depends upon points scored according to his rank, length of service and the size of his family. Thus the most junior young newly-wed will join the list at the bottom and will move gradually upwards, being occasionally overtaken by older, more senior colleagues. Beyond the criteria of rank and need, there is usually room for preferences to be argued—which design of house, which area, a date to take it over and so forth. But market forces—the ability to pay for what is desired—play no part whatever in the business.

The Look of the Place

'Quarters? They're all the same. I mean, if you've seen one, you've seen them all.' This comment came from an Army wife in her thirties who has lived in sixteen quarters during her eighteen years of marriage. Discounting the 'one off' small developments and conversions of individual houses within the civilian community, the traditional way of housing military families has been to build medium-to-large, self-contained estates, on or near the main bases. Most of them do indeed look pretty much the same. Although for many years it was considered desirable by the military to provide housing

for some of its personnel, it was not until after the Second World War that large-scale building programmes really got underway. In keeping with much of the rest of public sector housing of the 1950s and 1960s, most of the dwellings are utilitarian, box-like buildings, of depressing uniformity, set in neat rows, also of depressing uniformity. Road names reflect the Service which is housed: Drake Road, Spitfire Close, Mons Avenue. If officers' and other-ranks' estates are sufficiently close together, they may share a NAAFI shop and perhaps a post office, even a children's play area. They also share the same kind of front doors: everywhere they are the same, from the north of Scotland to the west of Cornwall, their plain, brightly-painted flatness proclaims 'Government Property' as surely as if there were a notice to this effect. Actually, there often is a notice—perhaps more than one: 'Ministry of Defence Property. No Unauthorised Entry.' 'Speed Limit 20MPH' 'Caution, Children Playing' 'Nos. 22–40a'. It is quite obviously institutional housing.

Every sizeable married quarters estate has a NAAFI shop, and entering one of these is, for the stranger, a return to the world of the familiar. For, inside what is usually an unprepossessing building—often a one-storey concrete and breeze-block construction—is a perfectly ordinary small supermarket. Most compare well with the average village supermarket in layout, choice of goods and price. NAAFI brand-label goods are sold beside others and shop managers are usually quite sensitive to changes in demand for particular items, as inhabitants come and go. They cannot, of course, compete with the big town supermarkets and those with cars use the NAAFI only occasionally. As in any small community, it is the hardest-up, without transport, who *have* to use the local store.

Other facilities to be found on most estates include a medical centre, places of worship for the main Christian denominations, some kind of other-ranks' social club, and buildings for the use of various activity groups—youth club, wives' club, brownies and guides, cubs and scouts, cadet forces and hobbies groups of all kinds. A play-group and/or nursery school will usually be found near the houses and a local authority primary school is seldom far away.

The whole is maintained by the ubiquitous Department of the Environment to a functional if *not* to an aesthetically pleasing standard. To be truthful, most large married quarter estates are externally ... ugly. But what are they like to live in? This is not a simple question to answer, for these communities have no civilian counterparts; married quarters are not like civilian estates, either of privately owned or of local authority houses.

People and Problems

Military estates are distinctive in the obvious way that none of the inhabitants follows any other occupation, and this arguably gives rise to the kind of narrowness of outlook which characterises other single-employer communities. The military, like the mines, or like agriculture, draws much of its young blood from the sons of its own communities.

Another peculiarity of the married patch is the limited age-range represented on these estates. The overwhelming majority of tenants are couples in their twenties and thirties with children. So, whilst there are children to be found in abundance, there are hardly any old people (occasionally an elderly parent lives with a military tenant, but this is uncommon). There are no extended families here either; no aunts and uncles, grandparents or cousins living nearby, and on any given estate, relatively few people will be found with family roots or ties in the surrounding area.

In some ways these are sheltered communities; there are no desperately poor people, few single parents, few black or Asian families to make special ethnic and cultural arrangements for; no head of household is severely disabled, or illiterate, or unemployed. There is no neglected or decaying property and very little vandalism—none of the more pressing problems which beset other public-sector housing estates.

But these communities also have problems. Some of the hardest relate to the fact that their populations are constantly shifting. The doctor who treats your illness, the girl at the NAAFI checkout, the woman who runs the keep fit class, the padre, your next door neighbour—familiar faces, all part of the fabric of everyday life—one day, suddenly move on, perhaps to be encountered again at another base, perhaps not. Genuine feelings of solidarity and comradeship seldom get a chance to deepen into real and lasting friendship, and while some people thrive on the semi-nomadic lifestyle, others undoubtedly feel a profound insecurity.

Other problems faced by military communities have to do with the fact that many of their menfolk are likely to be away from home for months at a time. Beside the coping difficulties experienced by some individuals, the community as a whole has to devise methods of not excluding wives on their own from most of the social life of the neighbourhood—without unwittingly encouraging liaisons between them and other men on the base. This balance is elusive, and although scandals give communities plenty to talk about for a long time, in reality many wives become socially rather isolated when their husbands are away.

Taking on/Giving Up the Tenancy

One of the biggest, and probably most unpleasant, difference between military and civilian tenancies is to be found in the method of their acquisition and relinquishment. A Service tenancy begins when the occupants of a house 'March In' and ends when they 'March Out'. If it sounds daunting, be assured, it is. The handover inspection of a married quarter is a ritualistic observance involving the submission of the family to the military preoccupation with extreme cleanliness and orderliness. Common sense hygiene and tidiness is turned into organised absurdity. The family vacating a quarter is expected to leave it in the same condition as that of a barrack block on the morning of the Admiral or General's inspection. Any shortfall will be paid for in fines (punishment) and although the Service*man* is held responsible in theory, in practice it is his wife who is considered 'dirty' or 'slovenly'. Some families waste little time worrying about it, but for the majority of wives, Marching Out of a quarter is always a traumatic experience. A local authority—turned SSAFA Social Worker remarked: '*I have lived in rented houses myself and at first I couldn't understand the panic that 'marching out' seemed to engender. It wasn't until I actually attended one, where the couple leaving the quarter had a disabled, incontinent child, that I had the remotest idea of what it could be like. With a tetchy President of the March-Out Board, it was a full-blown Day of Judgement. The tenants were called to account for, and pay for every crack, every stain, every smell, every breakage. . . . It's a major event. . . . A March-Out where the tenant escapes without having to pay for anything is a matter for pride, and where a man is complimented on his wife's cleanliness, all the neighbours will know. . . . The house proud wives love it—their efforts are recognised—but* I *think its grossly* "over the top".'

To give a better idea of the progress of an ordinary, uncomplicated March-Out, Terri Jeffries, a twenty-six-year-old Corporal's wife, kept a record of the seven days leading up to the event. These are extracts:

'**Wednesday 22 May**. *For past week or so have been getting house clean, like you would if you had visitors coming. Have got all the normal washing and ironing out of the way. Not many clean clothes now till after the move. Today washed kitchen, bathroom and toilet curtains. Started washing walls and paintwork. Did bathroom, toilet and landing. The lino around the toilet smells when wet. Daren [son, aged three] has just begun to use it on his own, that's probably the cause. Gave it a good scrub. This evening, got out the inventory and a heap of forms which say what things we've had exchanged and things returned, mixed up with forms reporting defects.*

Thursday 23 May. *Up early. Alan [husband] took over new quarter this morning then came home on leave. I ironed all the curtains before breakfast and felt sick.* [Terri is nearly four months pregnant] *Daren played up about going to nursery school. Washed his bedroom walls and did all the upstairs window-frames (getting bits of black mould off the metal). Alan came home after dinner and helped. The new house has three bedrooms and a good garden. Not in bad condition and due for re-painting inside soon.*

Friday 24 May. *Upstairs landing walls and paintwork. Tired and fed up. Ran out of several things in the cupboard, wasted time going to the NAAFI with Daren in the push-chair which he hates now he is a big boy, he screamed non-stop all the way there. Coming home I met Pam [friend] and went to hers for a quick coffee. Came back and cried. The toilet floor still smells and there are still black bits on the upstairs window-frames. Alan made our tea and I washed our bedroom walls, they weren't bad, but I did them anyway.*

Saturday 25 May. *Stairs and hall walls. Alan did most. The hall ceiling is stained where Daren overflowed the bath and it made a damp patch. I expect we'll have to pay for it. Had a go at marks on the carpets, got some out. Afternoon sunny. Had tea in the garden and Daren played. I went to sleep.*

Sunday 26 May. *Alan did the living-room walls and paintwork. I had another scrub at the toilet floor. This time I took up the lino and scrubbed the floor boards. They were awful, it can't* *be just Daren, perhaps the toilet leaks. This afternoon Gary next door was cutting his grass and did ours for us. I cooked a roast dinner, the last proper big meal I'll cook before we move. Tomorrow I'll start on the cooker.*

Monday 27 May. *Daren grizzly all day. Has a cold or something. Perhaps he's unsettled about the move, he can't remember the last one and I don't think he really understands what's going on. Cooker. All day, the kitchen stinks of ammonia. Alan checked inventory, we seem to have lost a Broom, Push, Head and its Handle, a Bin, Storage, Food, Rectangular and other things including a Mat, Bath and a Towel Horse 3 Fold, that we never had in the first place. Packed our personal possessions. Next door's telly's on, it's Bank Holiday Monday. Had fish and chips so's not to use the cooker.*

Tuesday 28 May. *Removal men came. Daren cried when his tricycle went into the lorry. Ante-natal appointment. The doctor said I looked tired but my blood-pressure was OK, worse luck, I think hospital would be heaven! Back home, realised we'd forgotten about cleaning windows. Fish and chips again. Washed and polished kitchen floor. We're sleeping overnight at Pam and Malcolm's. Shattered.*

Wednesday 29 May. *Up early, left Daren with Pam and went to house. Alan read out the things on the inventory and we went from room to room laying stuff out to be checked. Last minute dust around. (I sprayed some perfume on the toilet floor and crossed my fingers they wouldn't lift the lino.)*

11am. The March Out. *Alan in uniform, very smart. Everyone arrived together, they were the Families Officer, two furniture store men, the PSA man, a man from the Gas Board I think, and someone else. They started to walk round the housing examining things, but the Families Officer asked Alan to ask me to leave. He could have asked me himself. I went back to Pam's.*

They took about an hour checking everything. We were charged for some stains on the carpet, some blue-tak marks on Daren's wall, a broken outside light and some ring-marks on the dining table. Not too much. The hall ceiling wasn't mentioned. They said, though, that the cooker was only just about passable. Marching Out is so demoralising. All the same, I expect my next house to be as clean when I move in as mine was when I moved out. They haven't got a tenant for our house, it will be empty. I expect the cooker will go rusty. . . .'

A whole week of exhaustion and panic for a young pregnant woman with a little boy—and at least her husband was around; many have to cope alone. In this situation, neighbours are friendly and accommodating, but Marching-Out is treated as something that a family must do for themselves, an event that ranks somewhere between a trial by ordeal and an initiation-cum-membership rite of the tribe—like walking on hot coals. The standards demanded of someone like Terri Jefferies are out of all proportion to those expected on quitting rented accommodation in the private sector. A private landlord expects, hopes, that his tenants will leave his property undamaged and reasonably clean. From the rent gained, he anticipates shouldering the burden of minor repairs and cleaning before he re-lets. The Ministry of Defence charges 'an economic rent' for a tenancy which is conducted as if it were an incredibly risky loan of precious property to unreliable delinquents. If the whole self-perpetuating nonsense were scaled down tomorrow, the good tenants would still be good, the bad still bad, and the majority, a lot less distraught come removal day. . . .

*   *   *

'In' Groups and Isolates

Moving to a new base is a stressful experience, no matter how many times a family may have moved in the past. The military husband does at least have the continuity of his work, but his wife and children have to find their own way into the new community. New schools have to be started, with unfamiliar faces and different routines, an ordeal for the shy child. And the wife; what kind of social networks is she likely to find on the married patch?

The Street

The first group she would encounter would be 'the street': her immediate neighbours. One or two of her more self-confident neighbours might knock on her door and introduce themselves, but mostly she would meet people as they went in and out of their houses to go shopping, take children to school and so forth. At least a couple of the neighbours would be cheerful and friendly, curious to find out about her, keen to draw her into conversation, 'nosey' perhaps. If she chats, she would, through them, get to know most of the people in the street—by sight anyway. Before long, a house would change occupants and she would no longer be the newest resident; a fact that would make her feel more settled, more self-assured in her contacts with the neighbours. For many wives, the street forms the primary social group to which they belong—some will join no other. This is often the case with young women from traditional working-class homes where it is usual for friendships to be made on a neighbourhood basis.

If the new tenant is an officer's wife, the process of meeting the immediate neighbours will be very much more swift. Most will introduce themselves within the first week or so, and in due course, if she is not in employment, she will be invited to coffee at a neighbour's house. Coffee mornings vary from the cheerfully informal, with Nescafé in mugs and toddlers underfoot, to the terrifyingly formal, with the best china, the silver coffee-pot, the home-made biscuits and genteel conversation in the drawning room.

The Schools

As in every community, a focal point of social interaction is to be found in the schools and groups catering for children. Mothers meet other mothers at the primary school gates, at parent–teacher meetings and through their children's friends. In the United Kingdom there are no primary schools run specifically for military children, but near the bases schools will often contain a majority of Service pupils. Many bases run a nursery school, catering for three to five-year-old children and some will offer places to local civilian families also. Some kind of mother and toddler group is usually available, and an ante-natal and baby clinic will operate from the base health centre under the supervision of the local Health Visitor.

As well as being places where mothers meet, these groups also look for volunteers to help with the running of the organisations. Involvement in such voluntary work provides a way of making social contacts and satisfies a human need to feel useful and wanted. More often than not, however, it is the officers' wives who go into the primary school to hear children read, who teach at the nursery school, who run the mother and toddler group. . . . It is not that other-ranks' wives cannot do these things, but rather that an officer's wife will see her friends becoming involved and will ask, or perhaps be invited to join in. Other ranks' wives then tend to view voluntary work as 'not their scene' and by and large will become consumers rather than drivers of organisations and facilities. Of course, there are exceptions, particularly amongst the wives of older NCOs—although a high proportion of this group in the Navy and the RAF now live in their own houses off-base and fewer of them participate in camp life.

Women's Groups

An important social meeting place is the Wives' Club; every base has one and some, like the huge complex of Portsmouth, have several, located on the various estates. They are open to all wives, are usually organised by officers and older NCOs' wives and are attended by a loyal band of wives of men of all ranks. The 'loyal band' is often rather small, but a far larger number will be occasional attenders. Over the years in various Wives' Clubs, enterprising young women have sought to interest their friends in moving their clubs away from the old-fashioned-WI model (cosy and undemanding, with talks on handicrafts, cookery demonstrations and outings) to something nearer a Housewives Register model (concentrating on a greater number of cultural topics and controversial issues of the moment) but to no very great effect. There remains a smallish but constant demand for a woman's club devoted largely to domestic matters. For those who attended regularly, the club becomes an excellent place for meeting people with similar interests—and a recruiting-ground for allied groups.

One of these will inevitably be a flower-arranging group. The most skilled of their number will give instruction to beginners, and, if they are within easy travelling distance of a town, some of them will go to local classes and demonstrations. Once competent, they will assemble their floral creations in the base churches and chapels, the social clubs, their own homes and the Messes.

Another women's group to be found on all bases is the Thrift Shop which sells nearly-new clothes and toys, part of the selling-price of each item going to the original owner and part to charity. Again, the organisers tend to be officers' and older NCOs' wives and the consumers, mainly other-ranks' wives. The Thrift Shop performs a useful function, but both organisers and customers tend to form an 'in' group, and get to know one another, while other wives never go near the place at all.

Sports and Recreational Clubs

These are very much like the kind of groups to be found in any small town and are probably the least affected by the rank and status of participants. For generally it is talent and enthusiasm that counts, and people attend on their own, with a friend or with their spouses. A wife with an interest in, say, badminton or drama would find a warm welcome at the relevant club. Since specialist clubs wax and wane according to the numbers of enthusiasts posted in and out, it is sometimes difficult for new arrivals to find out exactly what *is* on offer. At most bases, soon after a family moves in, a representative from the neighbourhood who has volunteered to call on all newcomers, will appear on the doorstep with information about the locality and the clubs and facilities which operate. This information is updated and supplemented by Families' Bulletins or Newsletters—usually produced by someone on the housing and welfare side of the base administration—and by posters placed strategically at the NAAFI shop or the Post Office. Even so, it might still be quite difficult for a new arrival to find out whether the Keep Fit sessions still run, and if so, where, and whether there is a crèche. She may turn up as per the instructions in her pile of information only to discover that the instructor was posted last week and that a replacement has been obtained—for a different day at a different time.

Evening classes fall into a similar category. In theory, all bases run some educational evening classes which wives may attend; in practice, not many wives do, and numbers fluctuate so wildly that many a course collapses before it reaches its conclusion. But again, evening class attenders often form an 'in' group which frequently spans a wide range of rank and status, and, as with their civilian counterparts, some people will cheerfully enroll for almost anything—car maintenance, French conversation, coastal navigation, 'O' level English—in other words, the military has its own small band of evening class addicts.

Church and Youth Work

These are aspects of service in the community which again transcend rank and status. At one time, church attendance and its accompanying involvement in voluntary tasks was dominated by the officer corps and their wives. Now, it is mixed, and church and church-linked organisations are very much in the hands of devotees, who do the work for the satisfaction rather than the prestige to be gained. Thus, at one large RAF station a Flight Sergeant and his wife plus a Flight Lieutenant's wife help the Padre to run the Junior Church group, a Warrant Officer is, in practice, in charge of the Youth Club—with the Flight Lieutenant in nominal charge as his occasional helper. A Squadron Leader's wife is Brown Owl while a Sergeant's wife is Captain of the Guides. A WRAF Corporal is Akela, helped by someone's mum and two Flight Lieutenants run the Scouts.

Beyond these groups, which exist in virtually all military communities, individual communities will have other activities—a swimming pool, a riding club, a sailing club, a choral society, a brass band for instance—but the characteristic which all the groups share and which makes them different from those in civilian life, is that their membership is never settled, never stable. At one moment the drama club may have fifty members and be staging four productions a year to full houses, and then, within six months its key members may be posted, its standards fall and its membership dwindles to a mere handful. But while this is going on, the squash club may be enjoying unprecedented success and the newly arrived Education Officer may have signed up a whole roomful of young hopefuls for his photography course.

*   *   *

Isolates

No one can live in a community and be utterly untouched by it, but there are wives who find it difficult to attach themselves with any degree of firmness to any of the social networks which form part of the whole. In this event they become isolated and lonely: and the more withdrawn a person becomes, the more difficult she is to reach and to motivate into positive thought, let alone remedial action.

The 'classic' isolate to be found on all military estates is the very young, often teenaged, wife; underconfident, immature and with one or more children under school age. The Army, in particular, does recognise the difficulty which very young married women often experience in adjusting to life away from their own homes, in the strange environment of the military estate. Many regular soldiers are under the age of twenty-one and of these, quite a large number marry soon after joining the Army. Some do so because they are homesick and find life in barracks soulless, they long for domestic comforts and for familiar, unthreatening female company. And so, a proportion return to the 'girl back home', who may only be sixteen or seventeen herself, and, with the knowledge that the Army will provide a married quarter, marry—years before either party is really mature enough to undertake the commitment. Some of these marriages survive against all the odds, but many do not. Although the Army, with its larger number of young soldiers, finds the young isolated wife a particular problem, she is present on Naval estates and on RAF estates too. Perhaps not in such numbers, but she is there. Her misery is extreme: not long out of school, she may never have had a job, in many cases she has no qualifications, is not very articulate and is cripplingly shy. Unlikely to have lived away from home before her marriage, she is now cut off from the advice and support her own mother might have given her with her toddler or the baby. She is unsure about all sorts of matters concerning childcare; she wouldn't, perhaps couldn't, read a straightforward booklet on the subject, and is too defensive about her inadequacy to ask advice from anyone who might be able to help. Looking after the physical needs of her children keeps her indoors and uses up most of her energy; she seldom goes out, and when she does, she is sure that the neighbours are watching and talking about her. If a neighbour speaks, even to say 'Hello', she turns away in embarrassment. 'Official' callers—the estate staff, the boss's wife, the Health Visitor and others—are treated with extreme suspicion: '*Yes, I'm OK. . . . Yes, the children are OK. No, I don't want to join anything. . . . No, I don't need you to come again.*' Her husband is her lifeline to the outside world, and if their relationship has problems, or if he is sent away on detachment, that lifeline is severed. She becomes listless and depressed, out of touch with reality. The house and the children may receive little attention, and then, sometimes, the situation erupts. Perhaps the couple splits up and she goes home to mum: perhaps she neglects or maltreats the children and the Health Visitor finally discovers the situation: perhaps the neighbours complain about the state of the house to the Families staff—and something is done. But, more often, the situation never gets quite that bad. She muddles on somehow in a haze of near-despair . . . and no-one knows.

At the other end of the scale, there is another woman who is also an isolate. Though far better equipped to cope with her situation, she may nevertheless find it extremely lonely. This woman is the wife of the most senior officer on the base. There will only be one of him, and only one of her. The top man's wife is given a role to play in the community, but it is just that . . . a role, and it may be very far from her real self.

'*I'm afraid I wasn't awfully good at it, I think I got a reputation for being outspoken and "prickly"—actually, I'm socially rather shy, and I hated every moment—just wasn't cut out for it. . . .*

'*. . . You had to be interested in everything your husband did, but only politely interested; you didn't get to know anything much about the operational side—or the political, and that would have been interesting—you were only there as a figurehead. . . . I was President of the Wives' Club, I opened the Fête, I presented prizes at a Sports Day and so on. . . . Everyone was charming to me—but guarded. Even people I'd known in the past. . . .*

'*. . . One thing I found very hard was speech-making. I have in my time done some teaching, so you could be forgiven for thinking it odd that I found myself quite unable to string two words together to say "Thank you for inviting me as* *guest of honour to this luncheon" or some such thing. But teaching isn't the slightest bit like speech-making. When you stand up there in your best hat, they all expect you to be witty and entertaining—and* sincere. *As the only way I could get through half these things was to kind-of mentally switch off, I would have only the dimmest recollection of what had been going on; and that, added to the sheer terror that overwhelmed me every time I got up, prevented me from ever making a remotely passable speech. In the end I used to read a few sentences written on a card the day before, saying all the usual—"Thank you for this splendid—whatever— . . . the hard work and effort that has gone into making it possible . . . the ladies who arranged the flowers have done an absolutely marvellous job . . . and last but not least. . . ."*

. . . The only party I really enjoyed during our whole time there was our leaving party—I got blissfully and quite frightfully drunk. . . .'

Needless to say, this particular wife of a now-retired senior officer, is an amusing and formidably intelligent woman in her own right. But the inadequacy and helplessness which she felt on being pitchforked into a role which she neither wanted nor enjoyed, is by no means a unique experience.

Between these two extremes there will be other wives who, for reasons of their own, feel that they do not quite belong. Two fairly common examples follow. A husband, newly promoted and posted to a job where, for the first time, he commands a number of subordinates, is so engrossed in making his own adjustments to the situation that he fails to realise that his wife's status in a small community has also changed, and that she, too, may be finding readjustment difficult. She does not know how to behave to the wives of her husband's juniors: she does not wish to be stand-offish, but feels she should not be too familiar either. Making friends amongst her own newly acquired status-group may take time and the transition period can be lonely. There may be those who will protest that the promotion of a husband in the military hierarchy does not have such complicated repercussions on the status of his wife. This may be true on some of the large bases, for instance some headquarters units, but the smaller and more geographically remote the unit, the more sharply defined are the social distinctions between wives of differing status.

A second example, which outsiders may scarcely notice, can occur when a youngest child transfers from the local primary school to a more distant senior school or, worse, to boarding school. The mother than looses a major on-base focus for social contact. Unlike civilian mothers, she will have left behind friends made at ante-natal clinic, play-group and primary school, they will not have become her companions for many years to share the growing-up process of their children. When a mother arrives in a strange community and, for the first time, none of her children has to be taken to the local school or playgroup, she is suddenly thrown back on her own resources to find friends of similar age and stage to herself. Moreover, she is now outside the most important collection of mainstream 'in' groups.

Dissenters

Married quarters represent a good standard of housing for a reasonable
rent, and most couples will live in a quarter at some stage of their married
life. Not all find patch life ideal, but there seem to be a growing number of
wives who absolutely and unequivocally detest it. This phenomenon is new
(or at least, it has only recently been expressed forcefully) and for some
military men, it is disturbing. Wives who dislike living on the estates are
not in the majority, but they are often articulate and intelligent and include
many senior officers' wives, and many who are beyond, or have not yet
entered the 'mainstream' age and stage of patch life which centres around
couples with children. So what is it that this minority takes such exception
to? Criticisms return again and again to the issue of identity, and the way in
which patch life is perceived to undermine the individuality of the
inhabitants. This is expressed in several ways; for example, in discontent-
ment with the uniformity of the houses: '*I want my house to be different, I
want to decorate it how I'd like it. I want more privacy—a front garden with a
fence around it. . . . I am* not *like my neighbours, I am me.*' There is also
impatience with the subtle pressures to conform: '*Coffee mornings on the
patch are ghastly . . . but you can't refuse every invitation, it would be
extremely rude, so you go, and you smile, and you join in—and it* is *ghastly.
The conversation revolves entirely around trivia—diets, hair, clothes, furniture, flowers . . . and gossip. But I suppose it's inevitable in a way; we're not
stupid, but when it comes to the big issues in life, most of us think the same
way—so there's not much mileage for debate. . . . When I lived 'out' I used to
mix with a greater variety of people . . . I had among my friends a far-left
socialist, a boutique owner who was pretty far-right, a writer, a policeman's
wife, a musician's wife, a Friends of the Earth/CND/Greenham Common
Women supporter—I didn't agree with them all, how could I? But it was
stimulating. We did gossip too, by the way. Until you move back into quarters
as I've just done, you don't realise how—well how boringly the same everyone
is.*'

Another factor which causes some occasional resentment is the extension
of the rank structure to families. An RAF Sergeant's wife who lives in
quarters, but whose husband is planning to leave the Service: '*I accept this
rank thing, it's how it has to be. But it annoys me a bit when I know I'm as
clever and as well qualified as a lot of the officers' wives.* [She is a nursing
Sister] *Yet I'm not asked to help run the Wives' Club or the hospital visiting
rota. . . . At school my ten-year-old is in the top maths group, the other three
with him are officers' children . . . but they don't come round here to play—not
to the airmen's patch. Don't get me wrong, we're not treated as second class
citizens . . . but sometimes officers' wives are definitely condescending, and then
you wonder what right they have to behave like that. I'm glad my husband's
coming out. No regrets, but I'm looking forward to being someone in my own
right—not just a Sergeant's wife.*'

In a nutshell, these women want to distance themselves from the military. Though their husbands may belong, they want to remain on the fringes and preserve an identity which is separate from 'The Forces'. Mrs Sandy Gauvain, an ex-journalist and the wife of an officer who recently left the military, sees the 'married patch existence' as an—*'oppressive claustrophobic and anachronistic life led by women who have no status other than that conferred on them by their husband's rank. . . .'* It would be wrong she says, to suggest that the entire family population of the armed forces was in a state of mutiny. *'But I think there is an increasing number of women who are saying: "That's it. I've had enough".'*[1]

* * *

CHAPTER 4

Variations on a Theme: Different Kinds of Military Community

Having looked at some of the ways in which military communities differ from civilian communities of similar size, it now has to be recognised that military communities also differ from one another quite markedly. Obviously, each has its own particular 'flavour', but this notwithstanding, there are certain different *types* of community, which fall into distinct categories. Firstly, there is the mobile community (the traditional regimental model) which lives, works and moves together as a unit and, on posting, 'ups sticks' and leaves, lock, stock and barrel—and families. Secondly, there is the community of mobile individuals (as typified by the RAF station or any of the military headquarters units) where the life of the community is continuous, but individual families leave or join as they are posted. This, in Army parlance, is 'trickle posting' and is generally thought to be more difficult for families to cope with than regimental moves. For the RAF it is the norm. Thirdly, there is a depot community (characterised by some of the Army garrison towns, but most particularly by the Naval ports). Here, a large proportion of families live for long periods at a time while husbands depart and return as the Service directs. Finally, there are the overseas bases. Far fewer in number now than twenty or even ten years ago, families who live overseas find themselves in communities which more closely resemble the traditional military way of living than any others. They are geographically distanced from home, their social life is very much centred on the base, few wives are able to work and the community is generally more closely interdependent than those in the United Kingdom.

The Mobile Community

When a man joins an Infantry battalion (or indeed, a company of the Royal Marines or a squadron of the RAF Regiment), he becomes a member of an almost self-contained segment of the British military. In the Army he may move between companies or battalions, but most—or all—of his career will be spent within the same regiment. The regiment will be home-based at a garrison town, but tours of duty will take soldiers away—to Northern

Ireland, to Germany, to Belize, to other parts of the United Kingdom—as the regiments rotate to fulfill the various commitments, duties and training periods which the Ministry of Defence requires. A brigade can move as a whole, but usually one or two battalions go. And when they go, *everyone* packs and moves. Families take part in the exodus to major bases, (on average, about every nineteen months) but wherever they are settled, the men will still have to depart for unaccompanied detachments and courses.

The closeness of this kind of community is its greatest strength— but it can be stifling. Regimental families in quarters really do belong to the Regiment and to each other. The Unit Families Officer (usually a down-to-earth, fatherly man of middle years, commissioned from the ranks) will know all his families to some degree, and most of them will know each other. He will know, for instance, the families who live in what appears to be perpetual chaos, who quarrel loudly on their front door-step and not infrequently come to blows. When the situation threatens to get out of hand, one of the neighbours will ring or fetch him and he will calm the situation down before the Military Police become involved. The Families Officer will also know which of the soldiers' wives are, through youth and shyness, vulnerable to loneliness, and which, through temperament and experience, are likely to become key people in building and maintaining social networks. Families will get to know and, hopefully, to trust him, over what is usually a long-term appointment and will often approach him with problems where they might not talk to others.

In such a close community, few serious troubles go undetected for long. This is all to the good if the potential difficulty is grave, such as severe debt, child abuse or alcohol dependence; but often small problems like disagreements between neighbours or mild flirtations, which would pass unnoticed in other circumstances, can inflate to mighty proportions and cause intractable feuds. Within the regimental community of families, alongside the camaraderie and the mutual support, there is always some friction, always some people who are not on speaking terms.

By and large, however, the Regiment does seem to win a quite extraordinary loyalty from its families, and at the risk of being simplistic it appears that the higher the prestige of the Regiment (judged in terms of how difficult it is to get in) the higher the morale and the better the community spirit amongst the families. Take the Parachute Regiment for example. The tough élitist image of the Paras ensures a much higher number of applicants to join the Regiment than can be accepted. Nowadays it is not enough to be strong, determined and superbly fit. A candidate for the Paras has to be of good general intelligence also. It is not at all unusual for new entrants to have five or more 'O' levels. Initial acceptance means the 'Q' Course: for everybody—officers, other-ranks, the Padre and so on. This, as the BBC documentary series *The Paras* demonstrated, is a gruelling course, often uncomfortable, often unpleasant but remembered with pride and a sense of incredible achievement. It is a bond which unites every member of the Regiment and the pride extends to families too. A Lieutenant's wife: '*There are some terrific characters in the Regiment ... the social life is excellent, though there are rather a lot of stag dos. ... Also, there's not too much of a gulf between officers and men—it may sound clichéd but it really* feels *like a family.*' And a Corporal's wife: '*We go out a lot less now we have a baby, but my husband's bachelor friends are really good. One is our son's godfather—he's a drinker and a fighter but he's super with the baby. He'll come and babysit and play with him for hours.*' Most seem to agree that although the Regiment itself is a large organisation, within it, friendships are made and the interdependence, which is part of the men's working lives, extends quite considerably to the lives of their families in married quarters.

Nevertheless, things are changing a little. Ten years ago it was unusual for a married regimental soldier to live in his own house and not move his family every time the regiment moved. Today, a minority do so, but it is a growing minority and includes many of the more mature men and their wives who were a stabilising influence on 'the patch'. The official attitude towards this practice varies from regiment to regiment. Some look upon it as demonstrating a lack of commitment to the Army, while others take it in their stride as part of modern living. For the present, however, the traditional 'family' closeness of the mobile community remains strong.

The Community of Mobile Individuals

The community of mobile individuals is the least stable of all the different types, though for some, it is the most stimulating. It is a community in a continuous state of change, open to new people and, within limits, new ideas. On a base such as this—most RAF stations, most training units and military headquarters for instance—few individuals will serve for longer than two and a half to three years. But while particular families come and go, a kind of tenuous continuity is preserved. The role of the unit is one factor in this, so that a station such as RAF St. Mawgan will, through the Nimrod force based there, maintain a work force of a different make-up from that of say, RAF Honington, a Tornado base, or RAF Hereford, a trade training unit. Thus, in the RAF, on any given base, the ratio of officers to airmen, aircrew to groundcrew, experienced men to youngsters, will remain fairly static despite individual moves between bases. Communities like these are essentially rootless. They will have formal links with the local towns which are maintained with varying degrees of enthusiasm by different Commanding Officers over the years, but often they are no more than superficial diplomatic contacts.

Generally speaking, moving into a rootless community is actually easier than moving into an established one. No-one will have lived on the patch for *very* long and one is seldom the only new arrival. There are usually plenty of families in the same boat, struggling to find their way around, make friends, and (for dependants) to seek employment. Community activity levels are quite high though the fortunes of clubs and societies and also of informal groups of friends will ebb and flow dramatically. An RAF Flight Lieutenant speaks of the end of tour *'Everyone-we-know-has-gone'* syndrome: *'When you first arrive you meet a crowd of people which diminishes as time goes by. I mean, you stick with them and tend not to get to know too many newcomers. But there comes a point when you look around and find that the newcomers outnumber your original lot, and then you begin to feel it's time you moved on too. . . .'*

Although the community of mobile individuals is a relatively easy one to enter and a lively one in which to spend time, it does not offer much in the way of security. Neither friendship nor enmity has time to develop, most personal relationships will be superficial. Nevertheless, there are many people who find this kind of life intensely exciting and the perpetual moving almost addictive. An RAF wife after thirty-five years of marriage: *'We've always moved, all our married life. It's been two years or so and then off again. I dread the thought of retirement. Deciding where to settle is impossible; I don't feel strongly attracted to any particular place. For me, home is where you make it, it hasn't anything to do with geography . . . what's more, I know after two years somewhere I shall get itchy feet. . . . I hope I will be able to settle down when the time comes—but I have my doubts . . .'*

The Depôt Community

The depôt type of community is to be found in the Naval port and, to a lesser extent, in the Army garrison towns. The striking feature of these fully urban communities is the way in which the civilian and the military populations merge. Plymouth *is* the Navy, Aldershot *is* the Army. There is scarcely a citizen who hasn't a friend or relation serving in the Forces or whose livelihood doesn't in some way depend upon the presence of the military.

Married quarters are often occupied for substantial lengths of time; at Naval bases, five years is not an uncommon period for a family to spend in one quarter—and there are some who remain for longer. (Having said this, it must be emphasised that Naval families *do* move, and rather more frequently than members of the other two Services tend to suppose. The 1983 Armed Forces Accommodation and Family Education Survey calculated that the average Naval family would move two or three times in ten years.) These communities are therefore far more stable in composition than other types and are firmly rooted in their geographical area.

This is further accentuated by the tendency of Naval personnel to move out of base housing when they can afford to do so, and buy private houses in or close to the depôt town. Thus a situation exists whereby the depôt town stands at the heart of a community which actually extends for many miles into the surrounding area. With major bases at Plymouth, Devonport, Yeovilton, Culdrose, Dartmouth and Lympstone, the West Country is peppered with Naval families who have bought their own houses in the region and who have become part of their local civilian communities. In consequence, the population of the whole region has a high level of awareness of the Navy. Local TV radio and newspapers both reflect and engender an interest in the Service which is greatly to its advantage. The Navy, in its turn, is conscious of its image and goes to considerable lengths to keep the region's population informed about and, as far as possible, involved in their activities.

The strong point of the depôt community is, therefore, its sense of identity with the depôt town and the local area. Firm and extensive support networks for the families who live there have grown up over the years: they are kept in good order by constant use. For most households in depôt communities face long separations from the husbands and fathers of their families. This applies particularly to Naval families, for although soldiers (and a good many airmen for that matter) spend a lot of time away from base on active service, exercises and training, they are seldom away for longer than four months at a stretch. For the Navy, periods of more than six months continuous sea-time were becoming unusual, but the current reduction in manning levels throughout the military has led to a lengthening of sea-time again—even to nine months and more. This leaves wives alone to cope with home and children for extensive periods. On base, the Naval Personal and Family Service is available to help with problems; and tangible things, like the burst pipe, the transport difficulty, the children's health or their schooling can be, and are, dealt with efficiently and sympathetically. But there is nothing that can replace the psychological support of having a husband around when troubles arise. Most wives cope admirably, but a series of difficulties can place severe strain on the most capable of women and at such times a small extra problem can suddenly assume crisis proportions. A Naval Social Worker: '*Just a little while ago we had a CPO's wife who crashed her car and was in a terrible state. The car was a write-off; she walked out of it without a scratch, but stayed in a state of shock for a good three weeks. She had to be looked after by neighbours until we could get her sister to come and stay. It turned out that the crash was the last straw. In the fortnight beforehand, her eleven-year-old son had cut his face and arm jumping from a swing, her seven-year-old had been caught stealing sweets from a local shop, her central heating had broken down, she had lost—and then found—her engagement ring and she had not heard at all from her husband who was at sea.*'

The other perennial problem for the depôt family is that of re-integrating the returning husband/father. A Lieutenant Commander's wife: '*Think about it. You've had to deal with everything for the last six months. The kids*

have had measles and chicken-pox, the car's been on the blink again, your
mother-in-law's been in hospital. And his Lordship has been tootling around
the Caribbean. Then, suddenly, one afternoon, he's back, wanting to carry on
as though he'd never been away. Everyone feels awkward, the children don't
say much and it's all a bit heavy-going. Then gradually the thaw sets in, and
after that, the rows begin. . . . He shouts at the children for making a racket and
criticises their table-manners; he's cross about the new clutch you had put in the
car, he's rude about your mother when you gave up hours of precious time to
visit his when she was ill, and to cap it all, he gives you dazzling accounts of all
the super 'runs ashore' he's had in exotic parts of the world you hadn't even
heard of.'

In most households, after an initial period of intensely difficult readjustment, family relationships return to normal. But for some, the returning
husband remains an outsider. If he lacks the force of personality to *demand*
his share of the decision-making, he becomes little more than a temperamental lodger, and as his status in the family sinks, so too does his sense of
responsibility towards them.

When a ship comes in, everyone makes for home as fast as they can; but
there are always a few men who, after a day or two, begin to meet up and go
out drinking together. The depôts are full of pubs, and the pubs become
refuges for the lonely, the displaced and the desperate. If the community is
relatively stable, with strong social networks and time-honoured ways of
doing things, so too are the problems, the abiding problems of the sailor
and the sailor's wife.

The Overseas Base

Overseas bases quite obviously differ from one another a great deal: their
climate, cost of living, the friendliness of the local population, the distance
from home; these and other variables combine to make some locations more
popular than others as overseas postings. Despite these differences, overseas bases have important features in common. Most significantly, they are
islands of Britishness in foreign countries. They are close communities,
even by military standards, where few wives work and the base provides
almost all the facilities (shopping, education, health-care, entertainment)
which families use. Overseas tours still have an aura of glamour about
them—and in many ways, for many people, they are highly agreeable. With
few outside distractions, life revolves around inter-personal exchanges and
'socialising'. An RAF Flying Officer: '*You have a circle of friends who you
work with, live near, go to parties with, and, one way or another, see every day.
People join in more than they do in UK . . . I suppose because there's nothing
else to do, but also because they feel a kind of—responsibility to keep things
going . . . the feeling that if they don't bother to turn up for a party or
something, it might be a flop.*'

A sense of isolation is usually felt by most people at some stage of an overseas tour. The language spoken by the local population is often not English and sometimes that population is resentful of the British presence in their midst. The degree to which people *feel* foreign, and indeed, the degree to which they *mind* this feeling varies enormously, but it is always there. A Major's wife: '*Oddly enough, I felt more of an "outsider" in Canada, where we were posted on exchange, than during any of the three tours we've had in Germany. Perhaps I was expecting Canada to be more like England because of the language, and of course, it wasn't. The country, to me, had this vast, empty feeling about it ... and the Canadians we met were very nice, but basically, very reserved ...*

... Germany was different. I do speak a bit of German and I think that helps—and German culture and values are not too far removed from our own. So the feeling of foreignness was more exciting than threatening ...'

But a young Senior Aircraftman's wife did not feel at all comfortable in Germany: '*I don't speak the language so I do all my shopping on camp. I can't drive so I don't go off camp except when my husband takes me ... We sometimes go to Mönchengladbach—it's not paradise but it's a change of scenery ... Sometimes I think it's what being in an open prison must be like. I miss England ever so much—more than I thought I would. I never got on with my dad, but I even miss him out here. I watch English television programmes on the BFBS* [British Forces Broadcasting Service] *and cry ...*'

Employment, or the lack of it, is a problem on the overseas bases. Few wives are able to obtain work, and that which is available is chiefly on camp. Furthermore, the present scarcity of jobs in UK makes many families reluctant to leave their young adult unemployed children back at home. Overseas bases therefore contain numbers of wives and dependants who, in UK would be working or looking for work. If they have given up a job in order to come in the first place, they find their new status as unemployed military dependants unpalatable, to say the least.

An RAF wife: '*Secretaries, nurses and teachers have some chance of employment overseas, and if you're willing to do cleaning or bar-work, or shop-work with NAAFI you might be OK. But anything else ... forget it.*' Loss of employment hits working women very hard. It is not only the loss of income and concomitant loss of a degree of financial independence which causes unhappiness, but also the loss of a whole social dimension to their lives. Working women, temporarily unemployed through a posting to Germany, were unanimous that it was the sudden loss of colleagues or workmates, of a disciplined day and a structured week, of a sense of purpose and of individual status which upset them most. These feelings were shared by all—from a young woman who in England had been working in a pasty-making factory, to an older woman who was a dentist— and they are very much the same frustrations as those of men in the same position, coming to terms with redundancy.

But overseas the lack of independence and of individual status is magnified for the dependants of military men. For they have no identity apart from their husband's—or father's. They are known as 'Wife of . . .' and their entitlement to any facilities or services is through their husband. As the 1985 Survey of Military Wives indicates, this is widely resented. To rub salt into the wound, overseas, military dependants are subject to military courts. Juvenile first offenders who in UK might receive a formal caution from a senior police officer, are reprimanded instead by the military commanding officer. A forces family abroad simply cannot distance itself from the military. . . .

A feature of the overseas base which is often envied from the vantage-point of home, is the opportunity of travelling from the base to other nearby countries. From Gibraltar there is Spain and North Africa; from Cyprus, the Aegean and the Middle East; from Hong Kong there is China; and from Germany and the Low Countries, the whole of western Europe is accessible. Many families do *not* travel extensively, and reasons for this are not hard to find. To begin with, travel, anywhere, is not cheap, and one or two holidays with a family is generally the limit of what can be afforded. Time, too, is a problem, in that school holidays, which are the obvious weeks to go away, are the very weeks that relations back at home will want to come out to visit. Add to this the leave position for Servicemen (military commitments at any time take precedence over periods of leave, however far in advance they may have been booked) and the risk of cancellation inevitably overhangs all holiday plans. So, although some families *do* take off from Cyprus for that once-in-a-lifetime fortnight in Egypt, or a tour of the Holy Land, or go from Hong Kong into mainland China, most travelling is limited to day trips and one or possibly two holidays, not *too* far afield.

Overseas, the lifestyle of military families is more inward-looking and traditional than it is in the United Kingdom. For some, who can relax and enjoy what it has to offer, it is a marvellous interlude, recalled with nostalgia in after years and pressed for again in statements of posting preference. For others, particularly wives who at home would be working, it is a way of life which is anachronistic and restricting, tolerated with good—and sometimes not-so-good—grace, for the sake of family unity.

*   *   *

Within any community, certain sub-groups can be identified; in the context of the military, two sub-groups merit particular attention because they are almost 'communities' in their own right. These two groups are, firstly, boarding school children, and secondly, voluntarily unaccompanied husbands. Both are 'horizontal' groups, spanning all three Services and constituting a small sector of all military communities.

Boarding School Children

Imagine a married quarters site in the second week of July. The nearby primary school is holding its annual sports day and the long summer holidays are just around the corner. On the married patch, however, there are children on holiday already. They coast around the roads on their bicycles and eye one another warily. Though a few may have made friends during previous holidays, many will be newcomers, but by the time the local schools have broken up, these children—the boarding-school children—will have made each other's acquaintance and for the greater part of the holidays, they will form a distinct group or groups.

Boarding-school children may be highly intelligent or slow learners, they may be introverts or extroverts, well-adjusted or rather disturbed; they are by no means an identifiable type of child, but they share a common type of experience. Before they went away to school—usually at the age of eight, eleven or thirteen—they would have moved around with their parents and most would have attended several different primary schools. Since becoming boarders, their parents would probably have moved again, maybe several times. It is because of this highly turbulent pattern of home-making and home-moving that a significant number of military parents decide to send their children to boarding school.

The itinerant lifestyle of military families makes the education of their children one of the hardest problems which they have to face. The importance for children of obtaining school-leaving certificates to help them on their way to a job interview or to higher education means that they must remain at one school long enough to pursue a course of study and sit the relevant examinations. This, in practice, means that many families must partially split. Either the husband must move on without his wife and children, or the children must go to boarding school. It is not an easy decision; there are gains and losses whichever argument wins the day, but the boarding-school option remains popular.

Advantages are fairly clear. If the choice of school has been a good one, the child will gain a steady education with possibly the first chance he or she has had to develop long-term friendships with other children. Equally important, especially for children whose fathers are frequently away, is the opportunity for long-term relationships with other adults—teaching and pastoral staff. The Headmistress of a girls' public school: '*In my experience, girls from Service families are usually among the happiest and most well-adjusted of pupils . . . if they labour under any disadvantage, it is that in some instances their numerous changes of school can leave educational gaps which are difficult to plug . . . but mostly they do very respectably in their exams. The majority seem to have secure home backgrounds, and that stands them in good stead. . . . Of course, we have had Service girls with problems at home, and they've been very mixed up indeed—very difficult to deal with. Happily, they're rare.*'

Three military children who are happy at boarding school (at least most of the time!) explain what they think they have gained from the experience. Caroline, aged fourteen, who had attended six schools by the age of ten: '*I think it's much easier to learn when you feel settled. I mean learn properly—get interested in the subjects. . . . I was always in the top group at primary school, but every time we moved I had to kind of prove myself all over again. . . . Friends have made a difference. When I was at nursery school I always had a "best friend", but because of postings it was never the same person for very long. I can't remember having any close friends at primary school. . . . I was usually one of a gang. Since I came here I've made some "best friends" again. I suppose there are about five or six people I know really, really well—and that's nice.*"

James, aged 12: '*I know when my parents sent me to boarding-school they were worried about my education. I went to five schools—that's by the time I was nine. Everywhere the maths books were different, and just about everywhere we did a project on dinosaurs and a project on Vikings. . . . My mum went spare when we did Vikings again at this school! She said I must be a world expert by now! I think the education here is good because you don't have to keep doing things over again. Best of all I like the sport—we get a master who coaches us—not something like a lady teacher trying to take you for football.*'

And David, aged nine, who had attended five schools before he was eight: '*When I first came to boarding school last year I was a bit homesick. Actually, I was* very *homesick. Only for a little while, I like it a lot now. I know everybody's names in the whole school—even the cook's. The lessons are quite hard work, we don't have any "choosing" times . . . Dorm's good—we bounce on the beds, but don't tell anyone! . . . I like it when I'm chosen to show new boys round and tell them things like what the bells are for and where things are kept.*'

Security, a feeling of belonging, continuity in the school curriculum and lasting friendships, these things *are valued* by children who know what 'educational turbulence' is about.

Of course, it doesn't always work out. Parents usually select a school on the basis of cost, location and personal recommendations. After an examination of the prospectus and a visit to the school, the decision is made. It is, in truth, not a lot to go on when entrusting a child to the care of an institution. Certain schools may cater very well for one type of child and not so well for others; schools can change quite dramatically in standards and atmosphere over the years, so that mother or father's old school may not at all be what it was in their day. In short, there are bad schools; there are also good schools which are nevertheless unsuitable for particular children. There are children who find boarding a nightmare and there are parents who cannot come to terms with partial separation from their children. Sometimes, having chosen a school and entered the child as a boarder, the arrangement breaks down, causing much anguished heart-searching all round and ending as a net loss to the child's educational and social development. It happens, and some such instances are described in Chapter Seven.

The possibility of opting for a boarding education (with the aid of an allowance for which all members of the Armed Forces with children may qualify) has been available to military parents for a considerable time, but the kind of couples who are now taking up the option come from a far broader band of rank and social status groups than was the case twenty to thirty years ago. An Army Educational Corps Officer: '*In the 'fifties and 'sixties there were three main types of boarding-school parent—those with no choice, serving in British colonies where there was no provision for secondary education; those with a family tradition of boarding education—and a private income to pay for it; and those with aspirations to start one ... and they gratefully accepted the Forces Boarding School Education Allowance.*' Educational stability was a factor in favour of boarding schools then, as now, but at that time there *were* other possibilities to consider.

A retired Army officer: '*We thought about boarding-school, but we decided in the end the benefits of travel and living in foreign countries outweighed the disadvantages. ... Honestly, I don't think any of the four of them suffered educationally, but of course one can't be sure about that. In any case, it was a gamble worth taking—experience and personality counted for something then ... in addition to which, there were so many more places to go.*'

Another option frequently taken up by the parents of clever children in the 'fifties and 'sixties was that of transferring them from one grammar school to another as they were posted around the UK, and overseas as well, where Service grammar schools existed at all the main bases. This did not ensure continuity of teaching or syllabus, but it did provide predictability, within limits, of academic standards from one school to the next. Jane, the daughter of RAF parents, now in her mid-twenties, attended five different grammar schools: '*I went to boarding school for a year, but I hated it and came home again. Changing schools so often was difficult, but my brother and I managed ... I went up to Oxford, so that must make me one of the "successes" of the system ... but I had my share of disappointments. ... My first ambition was to be a doctor, but the moves played hell with learning sciences—I was always missing the bits of vital information ... my 'O' level results weren't good enough for me to continue and I had to concentrate on the arts. ... Perhaps I'd never have made a doctor anyway.*'

Today it seems that of the 'three types' of boarding school parents twenty or so years ago, only one survives—the parents who have a family tradition of boarding education and who would move heaven and earth— and the family silver—to ensure their child's attendance at the 'old school'. The other two categories, the parents serving in parts of the world without secondary schooling, and the 'social climbers' have all-but disappeared. The 'top' public schools are financially out of the question for most Servicemen without a private income, and the acceptance of the concept of a *boarding* education as a Good Thing *per se* is loosing its hold on the English middle classes. So why is it that a larger proportion of military families than before are using the boarding-schools? Talking to many 'new' boarding-school parents—who did not board themselves—it would seem that a growing number are not so much pro-boarding school as anti-educational turbulence, viewing boarding as a regrettable necessity. And although many are deeply ambivalent about the decision they have made, they do usually find themselves in sympathy with the aims and approach of the independent schools. They are, in fact, part of a new market which the independent sector has found for itself, and as such, this warrants a small, and not altogether irrelevant digression.

Families who, in the past, would not have considered a boarding education (including those of men from the non-commissioned sectors of the military and officers from lower middle or working class backgrounds) have apparently been attracted in recent years to the idea by a 'quiet revolution' in the boarding schools themselves. In her book *Private Schools and Public Issues*[1] Irene Fox charts the course of this 'quiet revolution'. She describes how the boarding schools faced severe difficulties in the 1960s. Inflation hit them hard, particularly the mounting costs of heating oil and teachers' salaries. This matter of teachers' salaries came to a head in 1974 when the Labour government implemented the Houghton Report on teachers pay recommending average increases of thirty per cent—which the private sector had at least to match. Between 1966 and 1976, boarding school fees increased by 200 per cent, and, not surprisingly, rolls began to fall.

In the face of this crisis, the boarding schools began to seek new markets. Most important among these were parents—grammar school educated themselves—who were increasingly attracted to the private sector as the Labour Party pushed through its policy on comprehensive schooling. But to tap this market, the schools had to change quite considerably:

'. . . *for, in addition to allowing some of their pupils to return home nightly, the schools introduced a more flexible system of exeats such that in many of them once or twice termly exeats yielded to fortnightly or even weekly boarding.*'[2]

And new parents were attracted. They were people who were unhappy with the large comprehensive schools in their areas, they were worried about 'progressive' education with its child-centred teaching methods, abolition of streaming and unstructured curriculum. In the private sector they sought better academic results, firmer discipline with the emphasis on the child as an individual, traditional teaching methods with small classes, and a fuller education. For their part, independent schools changed and updated their image:

'*The need to respond to the social and economic pressures experienced by the private sector, and the boarding schools in particular, has produced more changes than all the commissions, reports and half-hearted attempts at abolition.'*[3]

An important factor in the schools' continuing appeal to the 'new market' has been their emphasis on greater parental involvement in education and plenty of contact with children during term time. This attitude is as great an attraction to new Service parents as to any others, but it can add to their difficulties when choosing a school. Civilians new to the private sector are increasingly looking for a school close to home; indeed, Irene Fox found that, whilst academic standards are the main reason for choosing the independent *sector*, proximity to home is the 'commonest deciding factor when choosing a particular school'. She also found that, in contrast to the situation in the early 1970s, when around sixty-four per cent of boarders lived more than fifty miles away from their school (she cites the findings of Lambert: *The Chance of a Lifetime? A Study of Boarding Education*[4].) today, about three quarters of boarders live within approximately an hour's drive of school. This search for a local school is a departure from tradition and emphasises the different view today's parents take of boarding. Irene Fox again:

'Parents are not, in the main, abdicating their responsibilities to the schools and in explaining the importance of choosing a local school, they stress their desire to be able to attend various school events as well as the children's preference to spend time at home rather than at a local restaurant during their exeats.'[5]

But military families, whilst sharing these views, can find it impossible to take full advantage of the opportunities for contact and participation. Often they are posted far away, and this can cause parents intense sorrow and feelings of guilt—which in turn can unsettle the child. So it is, that whilst a growing proportion of military families are sending their children to boarding school, there is a great deal of uncertainty amongst the parents. Many expressed views similar to this RAF Flight Lieutenant's wife:

'I always said I would never send my children away to school. Never. But what can you do? There's no other way of guaranteeing one school through their 'O' and 'A' levels—unless we buy our own house and stay there, wherever my husband is sent. But that's something else we said we'd never do—so many marriages come to grief that way. Anyhow, we've started looking at schools. . . . I don't like it, I definitely don't see it as a perk of Service life, its just something that has to be. . . .'

Parents who feel as this mother does, put their children into boarding school with many reservations and worries, some of them better founded than others. Two of the commonest anxieties are, firstly, that of financial over-commitment and secondly, the worry that children will 'grow away' from their parents and perhaps also from brothers and sisters.

The first of these—finding the school fees—does appear to be quite a well-founded cause for anxiety. Military parents are subsidised through an allowance which aims to help parents meet the *average* cost of residential schooling in the private sector. As many parents are suspicious about standards in schools at the lowest end of the cost scale, a majority have to find the cash to make up the difference between their boarding school grant from the military and the actual fees to be paid. Military salaries are not huge, and this exercise can be painful; but if Eton is out of the running for most, a respectable, ISIS listed school of good repute and producing solid academic results is within the reach of a large number of Service families. However, schools may increase their fees at any time and by any amount, but the Boarding School Education Allowance like any other state benefit is only increased *after* prices have risen across the board. A school which might have been within a family's financial limits at the start of a child's education, may cause financial hardship before its conclusion. Likewise, a school entered by one child can become out of the question for a younger sibling—an injustice keenly felt in some families. Frequently, when the payment of school fees becomes a problem, a wife's job and income can assume critical importance, to the extent that she may be unable to move on her husband's posting, leaving the family split not two, but three ways. It is often argued that the Boarding School Education Allowance should cover at least seventy-five per cent of the *actual* fees paid, if the military wishes to retain the mobility of its families. And so it should; but it is unlikely to happen, since it would increase the cost of providing what is a controversial allowance in political terms, and it has already been seen that in other fields (for example the raising of married quarter rents) politicians in general are not as committed to the notion of the mobile military family as the military is itself.

Allied to the question of cost, is the matter of long-term commitment to a military career, no matter what other options become available. For, once a child is settled as a boarder and the family is in receipt of Boarding School Allowance, the father is virtually bound to remain in the Services for the duration of that child's schooling. Thus, the military creates the need for boarding education, assists with financial help to meet that need, and effectively ensures the continued service of men who apply for this help. An incentive for experienced men to stay in . . .? Or a trap?

The other common anxiety of 'new' boarding-school parents is that their children—who have few enough roots as it is—will be cut adrift from their parental home and will become emotionally independent from their family. This, of course, can happen, but where parents *want* family ties to remain strong, there is every indication that they do. In fact, it is noticeable that the most highly mobile of military families tend also to remain the closest, despite children's attendance at boarding school and fathers who spend weeks or months at a time away from home. It is probably true to say that families who can withstand the pressures of military life are very strong units indeed. The reason for their closeness is not hard to find. Nomadic parents do not have the opportunity to develop the kind of complex network of long-term friendships which, in today's society is the closest approximation we have to the traditional extended family. They do not remain in one place and with one group of people for long enough to become truly 'familiar', and therefore there is no replacement to be found for a missing member of the family: the family is incomplete and needs frequently to reunite to maintain its sense of identity.

Service children leaving home to go to boarding-school therefore leave a rather different state of affairs from those of their civilian counterparts (with the possible exception of the children of diplomats). For, at intervals outside their father's control, their parents will be directed to pack and move on. Parents' friends appear and disappear with alarming rapidity, the annual deluge of Christmas cards indicating a mass of acquaintances— potential rather than actual friends. The one thing which remains constant for parents is the regular contact with, and return home of, their children from boarding-school. By the time their offspring are into their teens, few if any friends will have known the parents for longer than their children have done, and none will know or understand them as intimately. Most military parents *need* their children as a 'fixed point', an anchor, every bit as much as the children need their parents, and for this reason, military families can and often do, remain extraordinarily close.

The problem of educating a Service child in a system where sequential learning is vital to the understanding of most academic subjects is one which has to be tackled by each set of military parents for themselves. Research into the effect of turbulence on the education of children is far from producing conclusive results but there are not many parents or teachers who would argue that it is a *good* thing, to be encouraged. The mini-community of Service boarding-school children seems likely to remain for as long as there is a political will to support the practice from government funds. If the political will should falter, there would without a doubt be an exodus of experienced men from the Services who have decided that a boarding education is the only way in which they can adequately counter the social and educational turbulence which affects the development of their children.

*   *   *

Voluntarily Unaccompanied Husbands

The final group to be discussed comprises married men who could be accompanied by their wives if they wished to live in their unit's married quarters, but who choose not to do so. Known as 'Weekenders' or, less flatteringly, as 'Beanstealers' they live in Mess accommodation and return home as often as they can—generally every free weekend. Numbers of men who opt to 'weekend' are increasing in all three Services, and though this increase has not been dramatic, it has been steady. It is a pattern of living which is more common amongst Naval men than those in the RAF, who in turn weekend in greater numbers than the Army.[6] This tallies with the proportions of men in each Service who are home owners, as does the fact that the incidence of weekending rises in the older and more senior ranks of both the commissioned and the non-commissioned sectors of the military.

A 'typical' weekender, therefore, would be in his forties with teenaged or young adult children, a working wife (full or part time) and a pleasant house in a part of the country which the whole family has come to think of as home.

Squadron Leader John Davison works at an RAF Headquarters Unit, where from Monday to Friday he lives in the Officers' Mess. The administrative job which he holds allows him to return home most weekends, and home is in East Anglia—a journey of over two and a half hours. At forty-one years of age, he has three children, two in their teens and a ten-year-old. The older children are at boarding school about an hour's drive from home and the youngest attends a local school. Home is a Victorian house, elegant and spacious and loved by the whole family. Though not situated in the most expensive part of England, the upkeep of the house nevertheless swallows a considerable portion of the family income. John's wife, Anne, has a permanent post as a school teacher and her salary makes a vital contribution towards balancing their books. Last year they had to cope with substantially increased school fees whilst a hoped-for reduction in the mortgage rate did not materialise. Finances, then, are tight, but not impossibly so. John describes the pattern of a typical week:

'On Monday morning at home the alarm goes at quarter past five. Fortunately, I'm an early bird and I've been used to rising at all sorts of ungodly hours to go flying. I get up and make Anne and I a cup of tea. I have a breakfast of sorts—cereal and toast—and by about ten to six I'm on the road. At that time of the morning the traffic's pretty light and I'm in the office comfortably before nine. A couple of cups of coffee and I start the day ...

After work in the evening I go over to the Officer's Mess. If I'm lucky, there's still some tea to be had in the ante-room. I don't know when they put it out, but by the time I get there, the tea is lukewarm and the sandwiches are curling up at the edges. Then I go to my room. It's not a bad room—about ten feet square with a window looking out on to the garden. It's got standard Mess furniture, but I've tried to make it a bit more homely: a portable telly, books, photos of the family and a pot-plant that looks as if its about to expire.

Between tea and dinner I usually have a bath and relax. Occasionally I play squash. At sevenish I change into a suit and go down to the bar for a pre-dinner drink. Most of the other 'livers in' do the same. We're a mixed bunch, but the married unaccompanied officers outnumber the single ones—from Monday to Friday anyway. Then dinner. Good food, well served, but if I'm feeling at all depressed, here's where it hits me that I'm living in an institution; sitting at a table in the big dining room. Sometimes a group of us will go out for a meal, or just a few jars at a country pub. It's nice, but none of us can afford to do it too often. So usually after dinner it's either back into the bar for a bit or upstairs to do some work. I always bring something back from the office—it helps me keep on top of my job, and if that's under control I can go home a little bit early on a Friday with a clear conscience. . . .

A couple of evenings a week I phone Anne; she tells me all her news and she reads the children's letters. Sometimes another of the 'livers in' will stop by for a chat and a coffee. If one or two more arrive we could bring out the brandy and sit up well into the night. That doesn't happen often, most evenings are very quiet. . . .

On Friday afternoons, I try to leave work a bit before five. As soon as I start the drive home I'm in a different mood. I look forward to the journey ahead. I arrive mid-evening to a home-cooked dinner—nothing fancy, shepherd's pie's my favourite. Afterwards, Edward, our youngest, goes to get changed for bed and I sit and chat with him. Then I come down and dry the dishes. . . . We've done this weekending bit for long enough now to have a kind of ritual established for Fridays. In the beginning we used to fall into the trap of trying to discuss all the week's events and problems in the first half hour. We were both tired and invariably there'd be an argument. Now we take things gently: only good news before dinner. . . .

The best Saturdays are the ones when our older children come home on exeat—then the whole family's together till Sunday evening. It may sound silly, but being apart for so much of the time, we really enjoy just being together, mooching about at home. . . .

Sunday nights, once Edward's in bed, are rather subdued. Business-like. We go over things we have to do in the coming week—Anne may have to take the car in to be serviced or I may have to write to the bank manager (again)—that sort of thing. But on occasions we talk round and round in circles about the future. In the end we agree to wait and see where I'm posted next before we make any decisions. Those discussions always end like that. . . .

Monday morning again. From the time the alarm goes, I'm back in the 'work mode'. So is Anne. Although it's early we whizz about, and our goodbyes are quite brief and cheerful—as though I was coming home for lunch. . . .

And that's it. It's not an ideal way of carrying on and I don't envisage doing it for ever, but it has its compensations. It does mean that in a small way you can have your cake and eat it. You can have some roots, your kids don't change schools, your wife can have a career. I don't think for us the situation is permanent. . . . I just don't know what the future holds.'

Although the increase in numbers of men serving voluntarily unaccompanied causes some concern in military circles, it is a trend that seems to be occurring in civilian life also. In the professions, advancement is often dependent upon a willingness to move, and weekly commuting—particularly to and from London is not now uncommon. The same is apparently true for middle and senior management executives in industry.

Family men, both military and civilian, who run their lives in this way hold widely differing views about the successfulness of the weekending arrangement. Few regard it as a long-term option. Amongst military men, the pragmatic view which John Davison takes about his lifestyle—it allows him to '*have his cake and eat it*'—is shared by a good many of his colleagues. But some, especially the older men whose expectation of marriage was never this, find it almost intolerably difficult.

It is difficult, too, for men who choose to serve unaccompanied overseas. Getting home is costly and time-consuming, but staying on base for an off-duty weekend when most of the other married men have gone home to their families in quarters, is no fun at all.

On the other hand, there are couples for whom living together seven days a week, twelve months of the year would be just as much of a strain. A Naval wife: '*For the first ten years of marriage Martin was away for two thirds of the time. We didn't like it but we accepted it—you do. Then he got a shore job he could do from home, he could even come back for lunch if he wanted. . . . I can't tell you how dreadful it was. We weren't used to it. Before, when he was home from sea I'd let him have things all his own way, knowing I could do them differently when he went back. But when he wasn't going back it was a whole new ball-game. What we thought was going to be a blissfully happy two years turned out quite the opposite. I don't know how our marriage survived, but it did. . . . He went to sea again and we moved out into the country. Now he has a shore job, and this time it works. He stays in the Wardroom most weekdays—sometimes he comes home, it's only an hour and a half. Weekends when he's not on duty he's here. . . . For us, it's just right. We lead our own lives, but we both rely on home and each other as an anchor . . . every weekend is a reunion.*'

CHAPTER 5

Family Problems and the Military Machine

The preceding chapters have shown that family life for the military man can be difficult. Given that this is so, one must nevertheless ask whether this has any bearing on the military machine itself. In other words, should the military care? After all, the Serviceman willingly chooses his occupation and benefits from levels of pay, job security and travel opportunities which would be the envy of many civilians. Lawyers, bank-clerks, shop-keepers and dustmen keep their private lives, private. Should military men be any different? On the one hand, what right has the military to pry into a Serviceman's conduct off-duty? On the other, what right has that Service-man to expect his employer to provide a comprehensive welfare service for himself and his family?

The answer is that the military *must* interest itself to some extent in every aspect of its men's lives. This is for two reasons. Firstly, military enterprise is, through and through, a team effort, and if the team is to function efficiently, the morale of all its members must be good. Moreover, since military men deal in a dangerous business, one weak link in a chain could truly spell disaster. Therefore the military *has* to be concerned about the man whose spirits are low and whose thoughts are not on his job. Secondly, the military often has to intervene in what may be termed 'private matters' simply because its personnel do not have very much freedom to alter their own circumstances. For example, a man may realise that his wife will leave him if he doesn't spend more time with her, but he cannot respond to this by reorganising parts of his life. He cannot, for instance, turn down the job in Ulster, work less overtime or move back home to Birmingham. He cannot even give in his notice and look for another job as he is bound to his employer for periods of years at a time. In consequence, a domestic crisis can cause a man intense anxiety as he struggles to right the situation at home without 'rocking the boat' at work. The military recognises this and makes provision for its men to come forward and discuss their problems — with a senior at work, or a specialist like a Families Officer — so that action can be taken with, or for them. The difficulty is, however, that no man likes to admit to his employer that he is not coping with some aspect of his life, and no employer is going to give career advancement to a man who has problems with life as it is, without taking on additional responsibilities. It is not surprising that Servicemen are often extremely reluctant to talk about family difficulties to their employer, yet it is frequently the military commitment that is exacerbating the problem. The situation can become dangerous when a man feels that his military service is rendering him powerless to tackle his domestic worries and he may lose concentration at work, act foolishly and land himself in trouble or literally make himself ill with anxiety. If this happens, the military cannot afford to leave him alone to work out his own salvation, for, at best they have an expensively trained team member who is not pulling his weight, at worst a man who could disrupt or even endanger the lives of the rest of the team.

Three examples follow: an accident, an offence and a suicide, all of which sprang from conflicts between military and family commitment which the individuals concerned felt powerless to reconcile. Such extreme consequences of unresolved difficulties are rare, but they represent the dramatic and tragic tip of a much larger iceberg.

The Accident

An accident can be described as an unfortunate event which is sudden, unforeseen and, by the time of its occurrence, virtually unpreventable. But accidents are *caused*, and in high-risk situations, accident rates can be minimised by preventive measures.

When an RAF flight ends abruptly in smoke, wreckage and tragedy, the accident is headline news and for a brief moment the dangers of military flying are brought home to the public. Because the RAF flies lower and faster using more powerful machines than civilians, the risks are higher than those associated with commercial flying. Add to this the need to train young pilots in a very intensive fashion requiring a great deal of classroom work alongside 'hands on' experience in the cockpit, and it is quite surprising that fatalities occur so infrequently. When they do, a full and thorough investigation is carried out by a team from the Royal Aircraft Establishment Farnborough, and it is usually possible for them to identify the ultimate cause of the crash. We say 'ultimate cause', because it is one thing to conclude that an accident was due to pilot error or to technical defects and quite another to speculate as to why the pilot made the error or how the technical defects were not discovered. In around forty per cent of cases, the accident is attributable to pilot error, but human weakness also accounts for a large proportion of technical malfunctions through servicing mistakes or design fault. Safeguards against human error take the form of repeated checks on men and machinery, signatures and countersignatures testifying to engineering work done and exact procedures for carrying out almost any manoeuvre on an aircraft, on the ground and in the air. But all these can come to nought through one worker's lack of concentration on the matter in hand.

Of every one hundred accidents investigated, there are three or four in which evidence of personal stress on key figures involved is so strong that it can be concluded (as nearly as circumstantial evidence can ever show) that it was a major contributory factor to the event. Where enquiries discover that personal problems were troubling an individual who was subsequently involved in an accident, this fact is noted and general recommendations may be made if it seems that lessons could be learned from the experience. But details of the individual, his circumstances and problems are never, ever published. The reason for this is a humanitarian desire not to hurt the families of those involved—there is nothing to be gained from publicly stating the opinion that someone's husband or father was so worried about his family that he caused an accident.

An RAF Flight Safety film entitled *Distractions* is shown at all operational stations in order to impress on personnel the importance of recognising and, where possible, reducing the irritations at work and the pressures at home which can distract air and ground crews. The film is fiction, based on fact, and it catalogues events leading up to a fatal crash. It illustrates the thoughtlessness with which people expect others to take on more work than they can manage, keep domestic anxieties out of their thoughts during working hours, re-arrange work schedules at short notice, cope with officious administrators and still play their parts as technicians, pilots or crewmen with one hundred per cent concentration and accuracy. Two of the central domestic conflicts which, in the film, contribute to the accident reflect common situations—real situations which have in the past put stress upon people who subsequently made serious errors of judgement.

The main character in the first of these is a Chief Technician responsible for overseeing and checking work carried out by servicing personnel on aircraft. On a busy station, he is continually pressed to get aircraft back into operation as quickly as possible, but he must always put safety first. Alongside this responsible job is a mature marriage going through a 'sticky' patch. The couple are clearly fond of one another; they have children who are now almost grown-up and the wife has assumed a caring role for her elderly mother who lives nearby. Her husband is due for a posting and this has caused some apprehension as his wife does not want to move. The day before the accident, the Chief Technician's worst fears are realised—he receives a posting notice to a distant station. That evening he talks to his wife; she is dismayed, he tries to cheer her up. He suggests that they could think about taking her mother with them, but at this, her dismay turns to anger: her mother is too old to uproot—it would be unkind—and besides, *she* does not want to go. If he has to move, he must go alone. Angry and upset with himself by this time, he finally agrees to see whether the posting could be changed. Thus, on the day of the accident, in addition to supervising work on the servicing line, he has an interview with his Flight Commander and follows this by explaining his predicament on the telephone to his 'desk officer' (the MOD officer responsible for his posting). An aircraft with what appears to be a minor fault is urgently needed by one of the squadrons; his wife is telephoning to ask whether he has made any progress with the posting request; he authorises a temporary repair when a closer inspection of the damage should have been made. And it is the failure of this part which causes the aircraft to behave abnormally when it is flown later in the day. As it turns out, the domestic crisis is not insoluble. The posting is altered, but not before the Chief Technician's preoccupation with the issue leads him to make the mistake that contributes to the deaths of two other men.

The senior of the two men killed is the second character in the film shown to be struggling to reconcile his domestic with his military responsibilities. He is a Squadron Leader, the deputy Squadron Commander and he has stepped into his boss's shoes while his superior is absent. It is literally a 'testing time' for him; the squadron is under pressure to meet its flying commitments and, in addition to running his own and his CO's jobs, he has also a troubled marriage with which to contend. His wife is in employment and is obviously a busy person trying hard to organise a home and a job with (it seems to her) a husband who helps scarcely at all. She resents the late hours he works, the meals she cooks for him which are ruined by the time he arrives home, the number of times she has to take time off work to attend to chores which he had promised to do. A man so dependable at work, so unreliable as a husband and father.

The night before the accident the Squadron Leader is late home after catching up on paper work in his office. His wife is exasperated and attempts to point out to him what seems obvious to her—namely, that he is being exploited. More work is falling on his shoulders than he can reasonably manage, but, career-wise he is vulnerable. This is an opportunity for him to prove just how capable a Squadron Commander he could be, and he is not going to begin by protesting that he cannot cope. Their argument ebbs and flows inconclusively but seems to leave the Squadron Leader feeling a little guilty at the way in which family arrangements are so frequently set aside. At any rate, when, on the morning of the accident his wife rings to remind him of his promise to take their daughter to her dancing class that afternoon, he is quick to reassure her that he will not forget.

The day, however, becomes frantic. A detachment is being prepared and the unserviceable aeroplane with the 'minor' fault is urgently needed. He insists that it be repaired with all speed and agrees to test fly that afternoon. He almost forgets to collect his daughter but manages to fit it in, returning just in time to take the repaired aircraft. He uses this routine trip as a training session, flying with a junior—and not too competent—member of the squadron. Both men fail to notice when the fault in the aircraft reappears. Seconds later it is out of control and crashes into the ground, killing both occupants.

The domestic problems of this character are more complex than those of the first and not conducive to a single solution. If he contrives somehow to reduce his excessive workload without seeming to admit to incompetence, he still cannot avoid working long and unsocial hours. If he offers his wife no help at all, he feels he is letting his family down, but if he offers help and then cannot give it, he *is* letting them down. If he insists on more time to be with his family, he puts his career in jeopardy—and lets himself down. He cannot win and there is no simple answer. Something has to give, and in this case, it is his concentration.

Although these characters are fictitious, their circumstances are only too lifelike. Widespread distribution of the film has elicited a favourable response from air and ground crews alike and it is often observed that the situations depicted are immediately recognisable from most people's own experience.

*   *   *

The Offence

By the nature of their lives, Servicemen are well used to observing rules and conforming to the values of the community in which they live. Serious criminal offences are committed only rarely by members of the Armed Services and conviction on a major charge brings rapid dismissal. Petty crime is more frequent and often drink-related. Taking and driving away motor vehicles, driving whilst unfit through drink, criminal damage, assault, these are fairly common charges levelled against Servicemen— usually in groups after a 'night out on the town'. No soldier, sailor or airman is allowed to remain in the Service if he amasses a string of convictions, and any brush with the law is taken very seriously by a man's CO, but, as in society at large, it is young men between the ages of seventeen and twenty-four who commit the greatest number of offences. Once past that age, most men settle down, and instances of criminality in Servicemen of older age-groups are relatively few.

When men with families do find themselves in trouble, a proportion of the (admittedly few) cases clearly show the offender being caught up in criminal activity as a direct result of being unable to solve personal problems whilst remaining a member of the military. Financial problems, for instance, which if disclosed would damage or even finish a career, can tempt a man to commit fraud or theft. Sexual deviants, and drug abusers too, find themselves unable to reveal their problems and, by having to live a lie, aggravate their difficulties.

The following case, unlike 'The Accident', is factual. It concerns a couple, Joseph and Barbara, and a series of offences committed over five years ago. It was Barbara who spoke about the 'Catch 22' situation in which her husband found himself, as a military man with sexual problems.

Joseph joined the military in the ranks after dropping out of sixth form level education. He had been achieving very poor results during a time of private worry when he had feared that he was homosexual. He became friendly with a number of young gay men, but his parents discovered this and intervened very firmly in his life. He received psychological counselling, altered his lifestyle and began to go out with girls. His parents, Barbara says, were delighted when he announced his intention of joining the military—a masculine occupation which would, they hoped, erase all memories of his fleeting homosexual tendencies. And indeed, he was not sexually attracted to other men, but one habit persisted—he occasionally and privately dressed as a woman.

On his first posting he met and married Barbara, a woman a few years older than himself who had been deserted by her first husband—also a Serviceman—leaving her with a little girl. The marriage seems to have been successful in most respects, although the couple were not very active sexually. Joseph found he needed help to become sexually aroused, and obtained this through dressing in his wife's clothes. As this happened in private and not all that frequently, she was not unduly upset by the practice. Two children were born and, outwardly, nothing was amiss, but gradually, Joseph and Barbara came to terms with the fact that he was a transvestite. Although she had not been worried at first, Barbara became aware (around the time of the birth of the youngest child) that her husband was developing a desire to display himself in female clothing. By this time her elder daughter was eight and the middle child was two, and she was alarmed about the effect that her husband's behaviour might have on them. Despite her protests, Joseph would dress up in the evening when the children were in bed, or in the day-time when no-one else was at home. On more than one occasion, Barbara came in from shopping to find him dressed in her clothes and heavily made up. After this, she also began to discover new items of women's clothing in the cupboards which Joseph had bought for himself.

For a remarkably long time neither Joseph nor Barbara seriously broached the subject, though both were becoming anxious that the neighbours would find out. They knew that, living in married quarters, it would be only a matter of time before the military authorities were informed and he would undoubtedly be medically discharged. In fact, when the couple finally discussed the problem, it was because Barbara's eight-year-old daughter had come downstairs one evening and seen her step-father dressed as a woman. They treated it as a joke, but Barbara was furious and gave Joseph an ultimatum: if he could not confine his transvestite activities to the privacy of the bedroom (as he had done in the early days of their marriage), she would leave him. This made a strong impact on Joseph; he did not want to lose his family and promised to control himself. They talked about the possibility of his seeking medical help in the civilian community, but they did not know whom to approach, fearing that the military would inevitably be informed. Finally, Joseph decided he would leave the Service 'honourably' when his term of engagement came to an end, and resolved to do nothing in the meantime.

He made an effort to curtail his dressing up, and Barbara believed that things were improving. Unfortunately, far from feeling more controlled, Joseph was a perplexed and unhappy man. He started going out alone in the evenings—he told Barbara, 'for a beer'—but in fact he was frequenting local parks and recreation grounds where he was indecently exposing himself. Barbara does not know for how long this was happening before he was arrested, only that when the arrest came it was both a nightmare and a relief. She remained loyal to Joseph during the weeks that followed, but she realised that his sexual abnormality would not disappear and felt she could not tolerate it indefinitely. Although his offence was not a major crime, its nature and the frequency of its commission spelled the end of Joseph's military career. And, sadly, the end of their marriage.

This offence was an uncommon and unhappy example of a military man needing help, but being afraid to ask for it. Also sad, but far more common is the following case, concerning an Army Warrant Officer. Jack P. was middle-aged, married with two teenaged daughters and a new, rather large mortgage. Beginning his last tour of duty with the Army, he and his wife bought an attractive house on the outskirts of the garrison town they had come to know well over the years. Their financial situation was difficult, but Margaret, his wife, had a part-time job, and Paula, their elder daughter, was due to leave college and hoped to work locally.

The first blow to their plans came when Paula completed her education and was unable to get a job. At first she was hopeful, but as the months went by and she was still unemployed, she became progressively more miserable. Jack and Margaret were worried about her, sorry for her, and didn't realise the amount of money they were spending in an attempt to keep her spirits up. Over and above their normal expenditure with their limited amount of disposable income, they were each giving her amounts of cash to help her buy new clothes, go with her friends to the cinema and to pop concerts—anything to keep her morale high and prevent her from giving up her search for employment.

Debts began to accumulate, and dealing with bills became a desperate juggling act. A mail-order firm from whom they had purchased household goods and clothing threatened prosecution, and although they accepted reduced monthly repayments, the debt amounted to several hundreds of pounds and seemed imposible to clear.

As a voluntary duty, Jack helped to run one of the community centre buildings on the camp where he worked. It was used by a variety of clubs— the Scouts and Guides, the Youth Club, the Mother and Toddler group and one or two others—and it housed a snack bar which did a brisk trade in coffee and soft drinks, crisps and chocolate bars. Jack would take the cash from the organisers and would replenish stocks; a non-profit making venture. Before long, he began to buy in bulk and at a discount. He discovered which club organisers failed to check their receipts and gave them inaccurate or illegible copies, and he pocketed the profit. It was not a fortune, it supplied him with spending money for his own needs, and, had he stopped to think about it, was hardly worth the effort, let alone the risk he was running to his career with his past record of high personal integrity. But he didn't think. Of course he knew what he was doing was wrong, but the amounts of cash involved were small and he felt that he had 'earned' them as a perk of the job.

An auditor, noticing the high turn-over of the snack bar, decided to take a close look at the operation—and inconsistencies in the accounts soon emerged. Events took their inevitable course: Court Martial, guilty plea, a moving statement from Jack's solicitor in mitigation of the offence, a sympathetic hearing from the Judge Advocate but in the end, 'Dismissed from the Service.'

In no position to get another job, this offence was not only career-ruining but life-shattering. Jack and Margaret sold their house and moved out of the area; they have not kept in touch with any former friends. If this had not happened, Jack would by now have been a respectably retired Army man, settled in the community of his choice, esteemed by his neighbours and friends. Perhaps if he had felt able to ask for help in managing his debts he might not have committed the thefts . . . his CO believes that the man's problems should have been picked up, and considers this case to be one of the system's failures.

*   *   *

The Suicide

Individuals under stress react in different ways, but when the stress becomes intolerable, a common result is illness. Anxiety is known to be a triggering factor in many physical complaints, from headache to stomach disorders, and often seems to lower resistance to infectious diseases. Anxiety too, can lead to clinical depression, a condition which is both debilitating and, *in extremis*, life-threatening. For, most people who take their own lives, do so in a state of utter despair. Very often there is no single 'reason' for this despair, it arises from the personality as well as from the life-circumstances of the sufferer.

Like every other calling, the military has its share of men who are susceptible to bouts of depression. It is a condition which is no respecter of age or ability—Admirals to Able Seamen are affected—but most men simply live with it. They may work harder, they may drink a little too much, they may become withdrawn and brooding; they may comfort themselves that many great men—Churchill not least among them—had to combat 'the black dog' of depression, and most do. But mental illness carries a stigma in the military which is arguably even greater than that experienced in the rest of society.

This stigma seems to emanate from a fear of unpredictable, and possibly dangerous or cowardly behaviour. The thinking would run that, if men are to work in situations where their lives depend upon the reliability of their fellows, they cannot be expected to trust a man whose actions they couldn't totally foresee. In the face of danger, it requires both courage and discipline for men to adopt the 'fight' rather than the 'flight' mode of behaviour, and one man's cowardice could undermine the whole of his team. So it is that the man with an uneven mental state is number one suspect for potential cowardice. Never mind that he is also number one suspect for extreme bravery. (Think of almost any outstanding war hero and ask yourself whether he was an easy-going, even-tempered, predictable man and your answer will probably be 'no'. It is more likely that he was volatile and temperamental, much-loved, much-hated, moody, and in some cases, quite mad.) Mental illness, or even a temporary instability is not conducive to career advancement, and it is not surprising that military men seldom ask for psychological or psychiatric help.

Suicide is fortunately a rare occurrence in the military, but there has nevertheless been a worrying increase in numbers over the last few years.

Robert S. was in his early thirties when he committed suicide. He was an energetic, ambitious young man with excellent career prospects, and his friends were stunned when it happened. The Ministry of Defence, quite understandably, does not release specific information about individual suicides; therefore the story that follows was gleaned, not from official sources, but from two friends of the family. Personal details have purposely been left vague.

Robert was a member of an élitist group within the military; he was physically tough and mentally quick. The military way of life appeared to suit him well and he seemed to thrive on arduous missions where he emerged as a natural leader. In his late twenties, he married Debbie, a girl several years younger than himself, and although they intended to have children eventually, they wanted first to establish a home and a life together. To most people they seemed a glamorous couple; good-looking, fun-loving, gregarious characters—great party goers, easy guests and generous hosts. Less charitably, some thought them a shallow pair, who constantly sought the limelight in a rather tiresome manner. Few people, however, came to know either of them well. Underneath, friends say, Robert was more than a little insecure and needed Debbie, for all her youth, to mother him. Moreover, he was sometimes quite morose—a particularly noticeable trait in the aftermath of intense activity such as a military exercise. In such instances he would throw his whole being into the event—and would usually excel—but afterwards would be left 'flat' and gloomy.

His obvious ability was recognised, he was promoted and given a post carrying a significant degree of responsibility. He pitched into his new tasks with characteristic vigour, and very soon began to achieve good results. He was, perhaps, more admired and respected than loved, but those over whom he had authority generally agreed that he had set out to make his mark and was already succeeding. Only one part of the new job was causing him problems and that was the paperwork involved. Robert claimed to despise paperwork, but it is thought that he did worry about the reprimands which he received fairly often for written work ignored or done in a slipshod fashion. He began to work longer and longer hours, and this, together with a full programme of active commitments, deprived him of 'winding down time'. He seemed tireless, but was probably close to exhaustion when, it seemed to him, his marriage ran into minor trouble. Debbie started to flirt with younger men, junior to her husband. She was not, by nature, deceitful, and it seems her flirtations were open and harmless—attention-seeking—but the behaviour was hurtful to Robert. He now had pressures at work and worries at home, but nothing went seriously wrong for him and those who knew him still thought he was set fair for a highly successful career, helped by a charming and vivacious wife. But life clearly did not appear that way to Robert. Possibly, his explosive energy had burned itself out and he simply did not possess the temperament of a long distance runer. One weekend, Debbie noticed he was particularly quiet; on the Monday morning he did not go into work, but drove out into the countryside and took his own life.

With hindsight, friends remember warning signs but doubt whether, even if they had known, they could have prevented the tragedy. They could not easily have persuaded him to take time off when his own peace of mind demanded that he keep abreast of the work situation the whole time. Similarly, it is unlikely that they could have talked him into seeing a doctor when the pressure began to mount. It would doubtless have seemed to him a weak and defeatist move, unmanly, unmilitary. . . .

Very few military men indeed actually seek psychiatric help, yet in the stressful atmosphere of combat-ready units, many suffer from stress-

related or psychosomatic disorders. Part of an interview with a Medical
Officer (the equivalent of a GP) on an RAF flying station follows:

> Q: Can you tell me the kind of problems that make up the bulk of your day-to-day work
> with Servicemen?
> A: '*Servicemen are a pretty fit bunch on the whole . . . most of what we do is short term stuff—
> injuries, colds and 'flu, vaccinations, routine medicals, that sort of thing. We have a few men
> with on-going conditions—I can think of some 'backs', we've got two cancer patients, a
> deteriorating eye condition . . . but, no, most of our work is done in two or three consultations.*'
> Q: On a busy station like this, do you see men suffering from the effects of stress?
> A: '*Oh, yes. All the time, it's part and parcel of the practice. Although we see more wives than
> men with psychological problems.*'
> Q: Could that be because the men are reluctant to admit they're having trouble coping?
> A: '*I should think that's highly probable. I don't think I've ever had a Serviceman who's come
> in and said "It's my nerves, doctor", though I hear it time and again from the wives. . . . The
> men are more likely to present with problems like difficulty with sleeping, chronic indigestion,
> general tiredness, concentration problems, headaches, backaches, dizziness—I could go on.*'
> Q: To what extent do you try to find out about the circumstances behind the presenting
> problem?
> A: '*Well, we do try. We ask about the hours people have been working—try and assess how
> confident they seem when they discuss the work. We talk a bit about the home set-up, but it's
> really up to the patient how much he wants to reveal. . . . We usually find, though, if stress is
> explained in an acceptable way—not putting the blame on the patient for the situation, but on
> the system, he's encouraged to be a bit more open.*'
> Q: What remedies do you prescribe?
> A: '*It depends. Often the poor bloke just needs a rest, a couple of days in bed. Sometimes we give
> sleeping tablets to re-establish a sensible sleep-pattern, sometimes a mild anti-depressant. . . . If
> the problem arises from a specific cause, we would advise acordingly, for example, if there
> were marital troubles we could explain about Marriage Guidance, if there were work troubles we
> could offer to speak directly to the fellow's Officer Commanding—I wouldn't go behind his back
> unless it was really serious. . . .*'
> Q: What about referral on to a psychiatrist?
> A: '*Yes. On occasions I do do that.*'
> Q: Do you meet much resistance from the patient to the idea?
> A: '*Well, again it depends. There have been situations when a man has become mentally ill, has
> got himself into a highly distressed state and in those circumstances he's usually relieved to be
> admitted to hospital—and it lifts a burden from the family too. But unless things are bad, it can
> be an uphill struggle to persuade someone that they need to see a "Shrink". The stigma persists
> you know.*'
> Q: Particularly within the military?
> A: '*Particularly within the military.*'

*   *   *

The accident, the offence and the suicide; the consequences at their most
extreme, of personal problems—sometimes caused, sometimes exacerbated
by military life—which the individual feels powerless to tackle. The fact
that private anxieties cannot be kept in a separate compartment from work
makes it difficult, and probably unwise, for a Serviceman to attempt to hide
them. But conversely, the fact that too many troubles or certain kinds of
problems can damage a career, encourages the Serviceman to 'play down'
any difficulties and not to confront them until he absolutely *has* to.

Safety at work, good order, morale, discipline and fitness (physical and mental) depend in no small measure upon men being able to devote a large proportion of their energies to the working task. This they cannot do if they are preoccupied with other matters. Everyone from time to time lives through personal crises—lack of money, marital disharmony, concern over children, bereavement—these are predicaments which touch us all. No organisation can shelter people from sorrow and no work place could, or indeed should, operate a policy of suspending from work those who are coping with severe or tragic situations. In fact, work under these circumstances can be a life-saving anchor for the sufferer and people thus affected can produce excellent work results. They can find that in making sure 'the show goes on', they can create an oasis of calm concentration for themselves in an otherwise disrupted life.

An individual living through a crisis is not automatically likely to suffer from reduced attentiveness at work *unless* there appears to him to be no prospect of an eventual return to some kind of normality. It is the person who can see no way through his problems, no end to the situation causing him pain, who is most at risk of succumbing to severe depression, inattentiveness and loss of a normal perspective on everyday events. The military man, however, is not helped by the ethos that men of his ilk are resourceful and independent and do not have private emotional problems. Emotion is something that the supposedly invulnerable military man does not usually care to admit to feeling at all.

The Serviceman with personal or family difficulties all too often struggles along, knowing he ought to *do* something but not knowing what, knowing he should *tell* someone, but being unsure whom to trust. The three arms of the military all have welfare services, operating differently from one another where families are concerned, but similarly in their approach to the fighting man. The military provides these services to help men deal with practical and emotional troubles before they get 'out of hand', but in the event of their doing so, to act on behalf of the individual, cutting through red tape and working out his problems with, or for him. So, what are these welfare services? Are they approachable? Are they effective? Could they be improved?

*　　*　　*

The Welfare Services

It is not the aim of this section to set out a comprehensive guide to the welfare provision of each of the Services—it would be too lengthy, too detailed for the scope of this book.[2] * Instead, it is intended to give an idea

*The University of Bristol Extramural Department produces a useful summary for members of its military Family Welfare courses.

of the general welfare philosophy adopted by the military and to consider how well it meets the needs of the individual soldier, sailor or airman and his family.

Through the Eyes of the Client

You have a problem. Perhaps it is marital, or to do with your children, or maybe you are in dire financial straits. It is not directly related to your work, but as you are a military man you have limited room for manoeuvre on your own initiative. If you decide to talk to someone, what results do you need to emerge from the discussion? Well, first of all, you need reassurance that you are being *understood*. That is why most people will begin by talking to a friend. Friends may not have any answers, but they will at least make the effort to understand, and that reduces the burden of feeling you have to face the world without an ally. Furthermore, unless you believe that your confidant is able to put him or herself in your shoes and imagine how you are feeling, you are not going to place much reliance upon his or her words of comfort and advice. So you find someone to listen to your problem, and if he or she seems to understand, you begin to open up. In explaining the situation to a sympathetic listener, you will define it more clearly for yourself—but you must trust your listener not to take advantage of your vulnerability. You trust him, or her not to mock, not to m: ke light of your worries, not to lose interest and not to relate your problem :o other people behind your back. You hope that however irrational you may appear to outsiders, he or she will be able to take your viewpoint and, if not share it, then at least appreciate it.

If this need is successfully met, you are already feeling a little less isolated; next, you need to be convinced that you can stay on top of the problem rather than being overwhelmed by it. Ultimately, the most destructive emotion produced by a personal difficulty can be neither anger nor grief but helplessness—the sense of loss of control which leads to alternating moods of apathy and panic. The bottom line is utter despair. Therefore it is important for your confidant to underpin your self-respect and encourage you to see that you still have choices, you still have control. (And however dire the circumstances, there are always ways in which individuals can take hold of their lives and alter course if they so desire.)

Having come thus far with your problem, you may need no further help; for once you feel secure in having an ally, and confident in your ability to stay on top of the problem, you may know what (if any) action you have to take. When it comes to the point, most people do. It generally involves being honest: stopping the evasion, the running away and squarely confronting the issue. Perhaps it is not such an enormous problem after all. Perhaps it is something which will reduce of its own accord as time goes by, or maybe it is something with which you can come to terms and accept.

Moving on to the next step; if you face your problem and decide that it is not a situation you can live with, you must take some action. You discuss the issue fully and calmly with your spouse/your children/the police/your doctor/your bank/your boss—the appropriate person or people—and, as a result, you resolve to change your pattern of life in some way. But if you lack the resources to make the change, you must ask again for help. Thus, your final need may be for practical assistance and things may have to be done for you—preferably at your own request.

To sum up, if you approach a welfare worker (military or non-military) with a problem, your need as a client is first, for understanding, secondly, for reassurance that you can stay in control of the situation and thirdly, for practical aid where it is asked for and is necessary.

The aims of the military in making welfare provision are not only humanitarian but also operational, and this colours attitudes towards client needs, so that the priorities of the client may be rather different from those of the military welfare system.

In the View of the Military

Defence spending is tightly controlled and money channelled into welfare services has to be justified in the context of military expenditure. The object of financing these services is therefore to *keep men operational*. It is accepted that in today's small, technological, peacetime Services, the career man will usually be a family man too. His problems will often centre on family issues and so military welfare will involve itself in these matters—in so far as it has to. But the primary aim when a man presents a problem, is to get that problem solved—fast. Welfare training varies from Service to Service, but it is probably fair to say that it is very task-orientated. Rather than beginning with a strong emphasis on understanding the client and underpinning his self-respect by helping him to stay in control of a problem, the military welfare worker tends to begin along the lines: What is the trouble? Define it. What can be done to alleviate it? How can I intervene to get appropriate action taken quickly?

This approach is magnificent when the problem is straight-forward and essentially practical. When it comes to getting things done, the military can be quite staggeringly efficient. Families can be flown half way across the world in next to no time and looked after with great kindness, compassionate leave can be granted without fuss, emergency housing can be provided speedily, rules and regulations can be set aside, expensive resources can be mobilised and the power to do this is invested in relatively junior personnel. When the situation demands action, things happen at a pace which would be the envy of many a local authority social worker. The drawback to the trouble-shooting philosophy, however, is that when problems are complex, symptoms can be chased while root causes are missed. Recalling the individual's three important needs—understanding, retaining control, and practical help—military welfare with its underlying aim of keeping men operational, tends to enter the arena at point three, looking straight away for things to *do*. Admittedly, this is less pronounced in direct work with families, but as far as the Serviceman himself is concerned, his need to be fully and carefully understood and to maintain control over the situation can too easily be overlooked in favour of immediate intervention to bring about a change of circumstances (or immediate rejection because intervention is not feasible). Although this may seem the most cost-effective way to operate, it is not, if it does not get to the heart of the problem, diagnosing it correctly, and it is not, if it discourages men with complicated or potentially embarrassing problems from making an approach to ask for help in the first place.

The point has been made that the military has to be concerned about every aspect of its men's lives. It spends money on welfare. The actual mechanisms set up to help men with personal problems are a unique amalgamation of traditional paternalism and modern professionalism. To illustrate 'the system' and how it works, imagine a young couple—call them Graham and Heather—with a typical problem. Graham is a non-commissioned officer, whose wife Heather, is expecting a baby. Graham is about to depart on duty for some months, and Heather, living in married quarters a long way from her own family, is anxious about the time ahead. There have been quarrels, and Graham fears that their marriage might crumble. Several avenues of help are open to the couple, let us explore them, one by one.

*   *   *

The 'Battlefield' Welfare System

The obvious person for Graham to approach about the problem should be his Divisional (RN), Platoon (Army) or Flight (RAF) Commander: a junior officer in command of a small section of men. In all three Services, ultimate responsibility for the well-being of personnel rests with the Commanding Officer of the ship or establishment. As he cannot know every man under him, the task is delegated downwards through the chain of command, each man taking responsibility for the morale of those working directly for him. This responsibility does apply from senior to junior officers but is formalised in respect of the non-commissioned sector, so that every soldier, sailor or airman has a junior officer who is required to act in a welfare capacity for him. There is no particular name for this basic military welfare channel, but 'battlefield welfare' is perhaps an appropriate term since this is the system which naturally emerges from active service. When the military task is being performed—'for real' or on exercise or training missions—men become very close to those with whom they operate, and it is logical for the officer commanding a single task group (as opposed to the more senior man commanding several such groups) formally to take on the welfare job which he would probably perform anyway.

So Graham, as a young non-commissioned officer, might consider asking for an interview with his Divisional, Platoon or Flight Commander, in order to discuss the effect which his impending departure on duty is having on his wife, Heather, and on their marriage. The officer he may see is likely to be one of two types. He may be a young man, possibly single, possibly with only a few years' personal experience of military life and in some instances, he may be younger and less wordly-wise than a good proportion of his men. Having passed through officer selection and training, he ought to possess qualities of intelligence and leadership which will inspire a reasonable degree of confidence in him from the men under his command. (For Graham would be one of ten to twenty or so men in the section, ranging from the most junior lad just out of training to one or may be two Senior NCOs. The exact composition of the group would depend upon the military job being done. Technical and highly specialised tasks, for example engineering or provost, would increase the ratio of NCOs to ordinary ranks within it, requiring more skilled men to carry the main workload.)

Although the young junior officer heads his team, and may be extremely able from the professional point of view, a lot of his men may be more inclined to talk to an NCO. If the Senior NCO of the section is a friendly, reliable man, he will tend to adopt a 'father-figure' role, attempting to be firm but kind in his dealings with juniors and seeking to provide tactful guidance to his officer.

On the other hand, Graham's officer could be an older man, promoted from the ranks. Many of these will reach Lieutenant Commander (RN), Major (Army), Squadron Leader (RAF) rank—some will go higher—but most will spend many years as junior officers. Being more mature in outlook and having experienced service in the ranks, an older officer may assume a father figure role or share it with his Senior NCO. (It is also possible, of course, for a Senior NCO to be quite a young man, say twenty-seven, and he may not be a family man either. However, very young SNCOs are not too numerous since 'fast runners' are likely to be picked up for commissioning.)

Back to Graham, who will have asked to have a private word with his officer or Senior NCO. He will probably be somewhat hesitant in explaining his marital difficulties, but it will not be like talking to a stranger as the man will undoubtedly know Graham quite well and will probably have met Heather on several occasions too. It is therefore reasonable to think that he will be sympathetically heard and fully understood. Indeed, the military would claim that the greatest strength of the 'battlefield' welfare system is that most of the men are in, or have been in, the same boat. But perhaps the military's faith in its officers' and SNCOs' powers of empathic understanding displays some complacency. It is true that Graham's problem will probably have been experienced in some measure by the officer or SNCO himself. He, too, will have had to face the difficulty of being separated from his wife or girlfriend at a particularly unwelcome time. But it is often the case that people who have confronted and overcome specific problems themselves, far from being sympathetic to others who fail to cope, are frequently less tolerant than a detached outsider would be. Moreover, once an individual has managed the problem in his own life, he is naturally inclined to believe his own solution to be the obvious and right answer for anyone else in a similar situation. (Think, for instance, of the ex-smoker or the successful dieter. . . .) Thus Graham, in taking his problem to a more senior person in the military hierarchy is by no means assured of sympathetic understanding, in fact, there is quite a risk of the reverse.

If there is a possibility that Graham will not be fully understood, it is almost certain that he will not be helped to stay on top of the situation. This is not the officer's or the SNCO's fault; he is not a trained counsellor but a man of action. He assumes Graham has come to him to get something done (probably to obtain exemption from the duty spell away from home—and maybe that is what Graham has in mind) but as Graham's circumstances are no more severe than those of many other men, he may well feel that he simply cannot be helped. He may even be irritated, suspecting Graham of asking obliquely for something he must know he cannot have. It is hardly surprising if his reaction is along the lines: 'Well, what do you expect *me* to do about it?' and if he gives any advice it is perhaps to tell Heather in no uncertain terms the facts of military life.

Unfair criticism? Well. . . . There *are* officers and SNCOs who will perceive the need to support Graham while he helps Heather to come to terms with a situation that cannot be altered. They will discuss with him how best he can reassure her that she will not be alone during his absence, will help him to arrange for people to keep an eye on her—friends, relations, military welfare workers, medical staff and so on, will reassure him that he will be brought home if she becomes seriously unwell, will perhaps even rehearse with him what he is going to say to Heather. . . . And will see Graham again, as often as necessary, not to do things for him but to give him steady, caring support.

Divisional Officers, Platoon and Flight Commanders can be helped enormously if the key administrative staff of the establishment are themselves approachable and sympathetic. The Master-at-Arms, the First Lieutenant, the Commander (RN), the RSM or the Adjutant (Army) the Station Warrant Officer and the OCPSS (RAF)—these and other administrators are often brought in to a tricky situation (and are sometimes directly sought out by men like Graham) and their response can be crucial.

The 'battlefield' welfare system is indispensable. It has great strengths in that it is logical, workable and fits in with the paternalistic, military-cum-public school way of doing things. Close daily contact between the junior officer, his NCOs and men fosters mutual concern and (usually) genuine goodwill. But the system can be ineffective where problems are emotional rather than practical and solutions are not clear. Officers in their initial training and on some 'in service' courses are given guidance on how to approach the welfare task, but it is patchy and could be much improved. Although not every officer or SNCO welcomes a welfare role, most will be called upon to perform one—probably many times in their career. It would surely be desirable (and cost-effective too) that on assuming a post with responsibility for a number of juniors, a man should at least be offered some intensive training. And this should include, first and foremost, practical tuition in counselling techniques.

The Wives' Network

The military places great emphasis on the welfare role played by the wives of its communities. In particular, it is believed that with Command goes a need for the Commanding Officer's wife to involve herself in the welfare provision for the wives and families of her husband's subordinates. And, to a large extent, this expectation is extended downwards from the CO's wife in a mirror image (albeit a somewhat blurred image) of the 'battlefield' welfare system.

As Graham's departure draws closer, Heather may decide to speak about her unhappiness to a 'more senior' wife than herself in the mirror-image hierarchy. The woman she chooses to confide in will probably be a SNCO's or an officer's wife; she may be young like herself, but if she is really miserable, the chances are strong that she will seek out a more mature, motherly woman. Heather will probably know her through some community activity—maybe she's one of the women who run the thrift shop, or perhaps she's on the NAAFI Customer Relations Committee or is Treasurer to the Wives' Club—an activity carrying some responsibility which will have impressed Heather and gained her respect.

When Heather confides her worries to a 'senior' wife, she is drawing on the resources of a network that is less formal and less powerful than the corresponding 'battlefield' system available to her husband. But having less power, wives are generally less preoccupied with action and more inclined to listen, understand and support. Moreover, as community involvement is undertaken more or less voluntarily, the odds are in favour of Heather's being given a sympathetic hearing.

The major strength of the wives' network lies in its ability to give support to women who need it, without interfering unduly in their lives. In Heather's case it would try to reduce her inevitable loneliness in Graham's absence and bolster her confidence in her own ability to cope. It must be said that confidentiality is not its strong suit, but provided she does not mind other people knowing how scared she is and how deserted she is already feeling, the network wives will rally round. She will be invited out, offered lifts into town, people will call on her and she will doubtless be given the opportunity to be helpful in some way herself. On one level it is a friendly set-up, such as one might find in many a small community: on another, it is a recognised, semi-official system headed by the most senior officer's wife available and willing to do the job. And the job done in the community is varied and important—from running the playgroup or the drop-in centre to occasional hospital visiting, from organising the new arrivals' welcoming scheme to making the tea after the mid-morning badminton session. The leading wives of the network are at the hub of a system dedicated to the creation of a strong community spirit and to supporting any of their numbers who are under stress.

Becoming a leading figure in the network is a relatively gradual process. It begins by being a regular supporter of various activities, continues by being voted on to organising committees and the like and, for the most committed, ends by being drawn into an inner circle grouping of 'wives who organise things'. Their husbands may be commissioned or non-commissioned, although within the group each woman will be aware of her social status relative to the others (according to her husband's rank) as well as her practical and intellectual status, according to her own merits. Community work as a volunteer brings certain rewards: a wide and expanding circle of friends and acquaintances, a feeling of being needed and a sense of closeness and common purpose with the other key volunteers. For some in the group there is the attraction of being on friendly terms with like-minded women of higher status; in old-fashioned parlance, of 'hob-nobbing with the gentry'—for the fun of it, from a sense of community, or maybe sometimes for the chance to cultivate a potentially useful friendship.

Without a doubt, the network is an immensely effective system—for those whom it reaches. But it does not reach all wives; it may not be much help to Heather if she is something of a misfit in the community. For the network requires some commitment, some initiative, however small, from the woman receiving support. She has to be in touch socially with other wives in order to ask for help in the first place. She has to possess a sufficient level of social skill to accept help gracefully and to express her gratitude—otherwise helpers will be put off by her manner and break off their contact. In other words, she has to want to belong, and in order to belong she has also to conform to certain minimum social standards of behaviour so that other wives will accept and help her as one of themselves. If Heather is young, underconfident, defensive and frightened of attracting gossip, she may not be able to benefit from this network at all.

Another weakness of the system is that there are simply too few women nowadays prepared to join the inner circle of the organisers. More women (and particularly the older wives) live off base and are unwilling to travel long distances to do voluntary work, and more are in paid employment. Of the rest, while most women are happy to be 'good neighbours', few are willing to commit themselves to too many hours of unpaid, and often unrecognised work.

There have been suggestions as to ways in which this semi-official system could be improved so that it would have a better chance of reaching the socially isolated, 'unclubable' wives—and also to prevent the system from contracting through lack of volunteers. The key to improvement must lie in raising the esteem in which these volunteers are held. They must feel they are doing a worthwhile job and must know that their efforts are valued by the military itself. Payment for certain organising work or for a number of designated, keen and able individuals has been mooted and could be helpful, but would not of itself solve the problem, since community work in any setting relies upon a good supply of capable volunteers.

A more productive move might be for the military to acknowledge and thank wives for the community work which they have undertaken as individuals. This could take the form of a written reference, to be given to a woman on relinquishing a regular voluntary job, describing the nature of the work and the manner in which it was undertaken. If the woman then returns to employment, the reference would at least indicate to a potential employer that the 'housewife' who was applying for their job had not only run a home and family, but had also been a valued community worker of proven reliability. Given accurate job-description, there should be no reason why every woman who took on a regular voluntary task should not be eligible for such a reference: the narrative would differentiate between those who had made major and minor contributions to the community. As has been said before, community work has its own rewards, but if volunteers realised that their efforts would not go entirely unsung, there could be an increased willingness to come forward. Equally important, the wives' network might be able to extend tactful, consistent support to the difficult clients of the system—to the angry, to the ungrateful, to the inadequate, to the unpleasant, to the disturbed—to the people who truly need help the most.

Padres and Doctors

Padres and doctors have traditionally served with the Armed Forces, and part of their function has always been to lend an ear to the troubled Serviceman. Medical and Chaplaincy branches are not large, but every military man is cared for by a Service Medical Officer (and many MOs look after families also) when he is sick, and just about every man at a unit is known to the padre—whether or not he and his family are practising Christians. Graham and Heather may prefer to confide in a man whose primary duty is to care; they may go separately or together to the MO in his surgery or the padre in his office or at his home.

Doctors and padres are professionally qualified for the work which they do, and it is difficult for laymen to sit in judgement on their competence. Therefore, although they are under the CO's command, they are rather a law unto themselves. As in civilian life, individual padres and doctors vary enormously in the way they tackle their work and in the regard in which they are held by their patients and parishoners.

The best padres and doctors are excellent. They combine a keen intelligence with a warm personality and a thorough knowledge of military life. They know the rules and regulations which govern their clients' lives but can take a more detached and objective view of them than 'career' officers or NCOs are able to do. Furthermore, they have direct access to the CO and their opinions carry weight with higher authority. There is, however, amongst this group, a number who are almost more 'military-minded' than their fighting colleagues. This is not meant to imply an addiction to drill or 'bull', but rather a very strong loyalty to their Service, which though laudable in itself, can render them less objective and on occasions, rather too eager to toe the party line. Only a small proportion of qualified doctors and ordained clergymen opt for a career in the Services; it is an unusual choice, and one which will have taken a lot of thought—and may have provoked responses of incredulity, ridicule or serious idealistic opposition from fellow students and friends. Having experienced this, many of these men are very sure about the rightness of their commitment and are extremely pro-military—sometimes to the extent that it dampens their perception of the less palatable side of the life ... Graham and Heather could rant and rail against what seems to them a harsh and uncaring military system which can separate a man from his wife in peacetime, when she is expecting their first child and is nervous and far from her own home—only to find that the doctor or padre on the receiving end of all this, seems actually to be a frustrated soldier at heart, and quite dedicated to the way things are. . . .

Family Welfare Specialists

The 'battlefield' welfare system, supplemented by padres, doctors and Service wives, has a long history. Families Officers too, go back as far as the provision of married quarters on military bases in significant quantities. The administration and maintenance of quarters was their chief responsibility, but over the years they began to assume duties in respect of the welfare of married quarter occupants. As their work took them 'on site', they got to know families quite well and were often approached by them for help and advice. By the 1970s, all three Services recognised the welfare role of the Families Officer and were actively seeking to improve it. Each Service undertook a major review of the welfare provision for its families living on or near the married quarter sites. As a result, each one took a different view about the adequacy of its existing arrangements and recommended different ways forward which have since been implemented. Nowadays, family welfare specialists exist in the Army, the Navy and the RAF—but are of quite different status from one another and are employed in differing numbers. If Graham and Heather should decide to talk to such a specialist, the expertise at their disposal would depend upon whether Graham was a soldier, a sailor or an airman.

The Navy has the most sophisticated system, developed following the recommendations of the Seebohm Report of 1973. The old Family Welfare Organisation turned itself into the Naval Personal and Family Service a centralised, professionalised service headed by fully qualified social workers. Centralisation is possible because the bulk of naval families live in or close to the Naval Dockyard towns. Three regional headquarters, at Portsmouth, Plymouth and Rosyth are staffed by Naval Social Workers recruited both from amongst suitably qualified civilians and from within the Navy. Naval personnel are sent on the professional CQSW (Certificate of Qualification in Social Work) course and return to work with families, operating in civilian clothes and without formal military rank. They are assisted by serving men and women of broadly Social Work Assistant status, who have the kind of supervision and team support which is found in local authority social work. As a group, the Family Service team functions slightly outside the constraints of the military in its area and attempts to bridge the gap between the Naval husband/father and his increasingly civilianised family. Taking advantage of the ability to centralise, the Service runs ambitious community projects and many integrated schemes involving local civilian populations. It is too soon to judge the system 'a success', indeed, the experience of supporting families under stress during the Falklands Campaign highlighted some of its shortcomings (a relatively small staff serving a large number of people, many living at quite a distance from the headquarters, making *personal* contact with all who needed it, *when* they needed it, impossible) but it is an exciting development. Exciting because it stands for a wholehearted commitment to mainstream social work providing a service for *all* its families—not just for ratings' dependants. Resources have been concentrated and strong facilities have been provided in the main centres of population. It is possible that, in the process, outlying units and families have been deprived of a service close at hand, but it is also possible that by raising the quality of service at the centre, outlying districts will still benefit through their access to it. Time will tell. . . .

The Army upgraded its family welfare system as a (halfhearted) response to the Spencer Report and has produced a semi-professionalised service, geared mainly to the needs of its chief client group—the young soldier and his family. The new system has introduced Army Welfare Assistants. They are of Warrant Officer rank, are female and in addition to their Army background, some receive training to CSS (Certificate of Social Studies) standard. (A less academic training than that received by a fully qualified social worker.) Under the command of a Families Housing and Welfare Service Commandant—an Army officer with no social work training beyond a brief 'in service' course to give him an idea about the discipline and what it involves—a Welfare Assistant will work with a good deal of autonomy and be encouraged to foster strong links with local civilian agencies. It is a service which depends heavily upon the capabilities of the individual Welfare Assistant. Naturally, the Army selects these workers very carefully, but they have a difficult job to do and sometimes find that they lack the 'clout' to do it as well as it could be done. They are insufficiently professionally qualified to carry a lot of weight with civilian and SSAFA social workers, and of insufficient seniority in the Army to impose their views on senior officers. A military service with more than just a nod in the direction of social work, it places mature, sensible workers on Army estates where they can help with community projects and visit families in trouble. However, their relative lack of professional, social and rank status means that they are not really able to provide a service for SNCO and officer families. And a service which is not effectively open to all, does tend to stigmatise its users.

The RAF reviewed its welfare systems in the Finch Report of 1978. It concluded that the RAF with its scattered stations and remote airstrips could not operate a centralised system like the Navy, neither could it adopt a semi-professionalised package like the Army, as it does not have a large enough target group to benefit from such a system. Airmen are, on average, more academically qualified, older and serve for longer than soldiers; on the whole, they present fewer problems—and their families likewise. When troubles do occur, they need to turn to specialists in whom they have confidence, whose ability and intelligence matches or exceeds their own. To employ staff who would fit the bill in large enough numbers to cover all RAF stations would be an unworkably expensive undertaking. So the Finch Report brought very little change to RAF family welfare, and it remains essentially an amateur business. Some Families Officer posts have been civilianised (and seem to be occupied in the main by retired Squadron Leaders), but their primary remit is still to look after the buildings rather than the families who live in them. On many stations, the job of Families Officer continues to be done by a junior officer who may receive no training whatsoever. The 'battlefield' welfare system and the contribution made by wives in the community are heavily stressed by the 'top brass', but in many instances both are thought to be patronising and unacceptably paternalistic by potential users. The Finch Report was satisfied that sufficient welfare back-up already existed in the civilian community to assist RAF families with personal problems and felt that no special workers were needed to bridge the gap between military and civilian agencies. Responsibility for creating links with local GPs, health visitors, probation officers, social workers, solicitors, head teachers and so on, rests with each individual Station Commander, his OC Administrative Wing, his Senior Medical Officer, Chaplain and Families Officer—all of whom have other jobs to do. Needless to say, the strength of these links varies from station to station and at any location over a period of time as key personnel are posted away.

The RAF has avoided the pitfall of having under-qualified, low-status staff which it could afford—but who could not perform a really useful task. However, it has done virtually nothing to improve upon a system that was found wanting by the Army and the Navy over a decade ago.

Civilian Agencies

Having considered the various avenues of help available within the military community, Graham and Heather could, like any other citizens, approach a civilian agency. The Citizens' Advice Bureau, a local authority social worker, a doctor, a lawyer, a clergyman, an MP. They may join a self-help group with other young married couples, attend preparation for childbirth classes, participate fully in local life—*if* they live close enough to a civilian community, *if* they know about the kind of help and support which exists in that community and *if* they know how to set about getting it. And even if they manage all these things, there is still the fact that the military man is not 'like any other citizen' but has a peculiar life-style which many civilian workers find incomprehensible. Graham and Heather might take themselves to a civilian welfare agency and explain their problems to a well-qualified, skilful listener—but a listener who will probably be profoundly ignorant about the modern military, and may even be biased against those who serve in it. They may well, to their dismay, discover the fact that most civilian welfare workers think of military communities as 'problem areas' and Service families as 'difficult'. Civilians from the 'helping professions' who practise near military establishments could do a great deal more to inform themselves about the realities of military life and the pressures associated with it.

To summarise, Graham and Heather, our couple needing support and guidance have several options in deciding where to turn. Someone in the military hierarchy or on the administrative staff, a 'senior wife' in the mirror-image hierarchy, a military chaplain, doctor or families officer or a worker from a civilian agency. Ideally, the person they consult should be not only a sympathetic listener and skilled counsellor but also an informed adviser, being conversant with the kind of life Graham and Heather lead.

But this ideal is hard to find, for helping professionals outside the military seldom have much understanding of the serviceman's life, whilst those operating from within the system are all too often undertrained, and conditioned to work in a reactive, 'troubleshooting' fashion. Graham and Heather's trouble is of a nature that defies being 'shot'. The detachment will go ahead and Graham will be on it; the survival of his marriage will probably depend upon the vigour of the support networks for Heather, within the community. Maintaining these, however, is an aspect of military welfare work that is all too often given a low priority. It is preventive work, and as such, is difficult to justify precisely in terms of money or man-hours saved.

As things stand, Graham and Heather appear to have numerous people to whom they could turn in times of difficulty, but perhaps this chapter has shown that some can be less than helpful, and on occasions it could be that *none* will be geared to aiding them effectively. It is a situation in which the service provided by both military and civilian agencies leaves much room for improvement.

CHAPTER 6

Understanding the Strain: The Effect of the Military Way of Life on the Family

Military families are as vulnerable as any others to the stresses of high-speed, high-tech, high-expectation modern living. But military families are subject to other, more particular pressures and while some families cope with them very successfully, some do not. These pressures arise from circumstances for which there are no real parallels in civilian life.

Military Ethos versus the Family Unit

Central to the understanding of the strain which the military lifestyle places upon a family, is appreciation of the way in which the military ethos conflicts with the present-day notion of man as a husband and father. When a man marries, he eschews his bachelor way of life and pledges a personal commitment to, and responsibility for, his wife and their children. Socially he is no longer one of a group of single men, he is now half of a partnership. As a fighting force, however, the military needs to maintain aspects of the 'bachelor-group ethos', even amongst its married men, because a spirit of comradeship and mutual trust within a fighting unit is essential. The crew of a ship, an aircraft, a tank need to be able to act and react together, almost telepathically if they are to be any use under combat conditions. Therefore, the military actively promotes off-duty relaxation as a group. Social functions, both with and without wives and girlfriends, sporting fixtures, training courses and detachments all serve to keep intact the close, disciplined interdependence of the fighting team. It is a fine thing, but families can never be truly part of it. In consequence, wives can often feel that a great amount of their energy goes into supporting male group activities from which they are more-or-less excluded.

'... *They have the Freedom of the City, and every year there's this parade through the streets—"flags flying, bands playing and bayonets fixed", something like that—anyway, it always seems to be a lovely day, sunny and hot. It's ... very emotional. There's always a crowd to watch, and it's ... exciting when you hear them coming in the distance—a buzz goes round of expectancy. When they pass by I'm so proud—my husband and his mates! I feel so much part of them, I want to be out there marching too—and I feel sad that no way can I ever do that. . . . It hammers home that when it comes down to it, Army wives are spectators. . . . The men have this incredibly close rapport with each other whatever they're doing—parades, exercises, you name it—and the wives are left out. . . . Sometimes it makes me jealous, it really does. . . .'*

This feeling of exclusion is seldom an all-pervading one, but is likely to be triggered quite unexpectedly by some event which seems to a woman to demonstrate that her husband's first loyalty lies with the military rather than with his family. In talking to many wives, however, it is striking to note that it is not the 'big' things, the predictable duties—like going off to trouble spots, or unaccompanied tours, or training courses—that cause the most resentment, but actions which give the impression (correctly or incorrectly) that their husbands are seeking the company of their fellows in preference to that of their families. And the fact that the military emphasises the importance of *esprit de corps*, on and off duty, can make wives feel guilty and selfish if they seem to be undermining it.

Belinda J. a Naval Officer's wife: '*When our son was born my husband was away for the day, playing squash. It was three days before he* [the baby] *was due but we knew it could be any time, and he still went off in the morning to play the match. He never* thought *about pulling out—it would have been letting the side down. And it didn't occur to me to make a fuss about it. Not at the time. It was afterwards I was angry. . . . My next door neighbour drove me into hospital, and they asked me where by husband was. When I said "Two hundred miles away, playing squash", they looked at me in utter disbelief. . . . I know it wasn't that the squash match meant more to him than me and the baby, but when it was visiting time in the evening and he* still *wasn't back, that's what it felt like. I wept buckets. He finally arrived at about eleven o'clock at night, and I cried again. I was so happy but so cross—all at the same time . . . Looking back though, what gets to me is the way we both just accepted that the Navy had to come first—even with a stupid, trivial thing like a squash match.'*

The close relationship between men serving together can come between married couples—particularly newly married couples, where a young wife has had little time to get used to military life and can feel bewildered as well as excluded. Going out 'with the lads' is a common enough pastime amongst young men anywhere in our society, and usually, when a man marries, separation from his bachelor friends is a gradual process, punctuated by the odd reunion of male companions. Frequently it is the arrival of a baby which finally distances the young married man from his single friends. Henceforth, friendships tend to be made as a couple, with other couples. In the military, however, groups of men contemporary in age and rank who are working together, tend to stick together socially too—and that includes those of the group who are married. Furthermore, until the majority of the group are married men, the bachelor ethos will dominate it.

Wives and girlfriends will be hard pressed to pull their menfolk away from the group, few will try.

Carol, a Private's wife: *'We've been married two years now and we've got a little girl. Les was one of the first blokes in his lot to get married. Until about six months ago, most of them were single, living in barracks. They're good blokes actually, it's just when they're out together they sometimes go over the top—you know, silly. Childish. When they've had a bit to drink they get rowdy, and unless you're the sort of girl that likes that, there comes a time when you want out. . . . It's bad enough if you're on camp or at a pub but quite often, if you're married, it's in your house. A whole load of them turn up with piles of beer cans and expect to take over your lounge—and your husband doesn't care. They don't think they might wake the baby up . . . I can tell you I've been mad at him . . . Lately it's fallen off a bit. Three of the blokes have got married themselves and another one who's been married for a while, his wife's just had a baby.'*

Although this kind of occurrence is to be found in civilian groups too, in the military community the bachelor group does possess great tenacity, and of course it also operates amongst the young commissioned men—in very similar fashion.

Sue, a Flying Officer's wife: *'I should say about half Andy's friends are married and half single. Most of them have got steady girls now. But there's no knowing when the doorbell will ring and half a dozen fellas will be standing on the doorstep with great big gormless grins and armsful of booze. And you can bet your life they're starving hungry. . . . They tell me how wonderful I am—but I reckon there are times when I need my head examining.'*

Most wives recounting this kind of experience do so with a touch of good-humoured resignation, but humour tends to go out of the situation when children enter the picture. If a woman begins to believe that her husband is putting his commitment to the military above his commitment to their children, she can become very bitter, very angry indeed.

'The way I look at it, we chose the life and if it causes us discomfort, well so be it. But the children didn't choose it—the poor little sods just have to put up with it. . . . I'm going to fight all I have to to give them a good childhood.' This Army Sergeant's wife went on: *'My Dave's a rugby player—in the Battalion side, that's supposed to be a great honour. . . . There was a little concert they put on at Laura's school, she was playing her recorder and doing a reading, and we were going to go. Of course, there was rugby that Wednesday wasn't there? Well he should have been home in plenty of time, but oh no, he had to stay on afterwards for the beer. It got so late I went on my own for Laura's sake, but I missed the first ten minutes when she did the reading and she was ever so upset. . . . She told her friends her dad was coming. He was sorry when we got home, but sorry doesn't make it better does it? I know if the same thing happened again he'd act the same way. . . .'*

Another aspect of the clash between military and family commitment concerns money. Relaxation time with colleagues invariably includes eating and drinking together, and this costs money. Although the military encourages this expression of comradeship, it does not foot the bill. In the Senior NCO's and Officers' Messes (and Naval Wardrooms), evening functions of various kinds are regularly held, some limited to military personnel, some extending invitations to 'their ladies' and guests. The most formal and lavish occasions are dinners, cocktail parties and an annual ball. The Mess silver decorates the tables, huge arrangements of fresh flowers stand in the main rooms, music plays and numerous staff are on hand to serve the excellent food and drink and generally take care of the guests. Impressive occasions, even for seasoned attenders. But not cheap; and not optional. Men are not expected to attend every single Mess function, but they are certainly expected to be present at the more important (and expensive) events and a selection of the minor ones.

An RAF Officer's wife relates: '*When our daughter was about ten, she developed a passion for horses and she desperately wanted to learn to ride. It was going to cost in the region of five pounds a week. We thought about it very carefully—we'd just bought a car, we had a hefty mortgage—money was tight. In the end we had to tell her "no". We just couldn't afford it. She took it very well . . . Do you know, the very next week, Roger* [husband] *came home saying we had to go to a special Battle of Britain Dinner—a high-powered thing. It wasn't in our Mess, we had to drive there and stay over-night. The whole thing cost us about fifty pounds in all. . . . Maybe that's not extortionate for the kind of occasion it was, but we didn't exactly ask to go. . . . I remember, all through the evening, I kept thinking "We're spending more on this than we'd need for a whole term's* riding lessons" . . .'

Almost any military wife could cite instances where the Service demanded—and got—time, enthusiasm, energy and cash expenditure from her husband which she feels should have been directed towards the family. Amongst husbands, feelings appear to be more mixed. Many believe that if there is a clash of loyalties the military must come first, not only because in the last resort the military can command it, but also because they think it is in the family's long-term interests that it should be so.

A Fleet Air Arm Senior Rate and his wife put forward two perspectives on the same issue. An incident that had occurred in the recent past had caused considerable friction between them—it was still a touchy subject. (The following dialogue was not tape-recorded but taken down in note form and may not be 'word perfect'.)

Keith: '*There was a short course which technicians like myself had to do. I was given the chance of going on the first one they ran, right? But it meant putting off some leave. I know I could have asked to go on a later one, but it didn't seem like a good idea. Why? Because I'm in the Navy for—well for most of my working life I hope. Yes, I'm looking for promotion, but not just for me, for Anna and the kids too . . .*'

Anna: *'We had a holiday booked. Not just planned; booked. We had actually paid the deposit. He doesn't tell you how much he'd been away before that—a heck of a lot . . . I was absolutely determined that when his leave came up we were going to go away as a family and have some sunshine. . . . The boys* [aged eight and six] *hardly see their dad except when he's rushing in and out, working funny hours—and there's always some panic . . . We really needed that holiday. After all, it wasn't as though it was the* only *course, he could have done it later.'*

Keith: *'Yes, but if I'd asked for that, my name would have gone to the bottom of the list and other blokes would have done it in front of me. Then they'd have known things I didn't, and I wouldn't have felt comfortable with that.'*

Anna: *'Come off it, you were flattered your name was down for the first course and you wanted to live up to the image of the "eager beaver".'*

Keith: *'That's not fair—But what if I did? . . . If I get on in the Navy, we'll all have a better life.'*

Anna: *'We could have had a better life* then *if we'd gone to Spain like we planned.'*

Keith: *'Well you say it was booked, but it was done a long way in advance and we were insured against cancellation. We re-arranged. We went the following Autumn didn't we?'*

Anna: *'Yes, and it was lovely, but the children had to have two weeks off school at the beginning of the year when they were in new classes. And we had a miserable Summer. You weren't around, and the weather was dreadful, and I was really cheesed off.'*

Keith: *'I know. I still think I did the right thing though. It'll pay dividends in the long run.'*

Anna: *'Perhaps. But if things had gone on much longer like they were, there wouldn't have been any long run where our marriage was concerned.'*

It would be wrong to imagine that military men themselves are never torn, never feel resentment at demands made on them which cannot be refused. An officer in his mid-thirties who has not long completed a tour of duty as a Personal Staff Officer to a very senior military man (a 'plum' job in which a relatively young man can get to know the workings of high office) describes how the job has caused him to question his future with the Armed Forces:

'Being a PSO has made me think; made me think very hard about how to play this game—and whether the game's worth the playing. . . . I was an extremely keen young officer. I was also lucky—the right place at the right time—and I was obviously delighted to get the PSO post. . . . I worked in Whitehall for a very charming, but hard-working, peronally ambitious man. You work the same hours as your master—longer in fact. Come hell or high water. I was lucky if I got home before ten or eleven in the evening. Every evening. Adam was five at the beginning of the tour and Sophie was not quite

two. . . . I'd go for days and days not seeing either of them. I can remember exactly the moment when I began to have doubts about my ambitions in the Service. Sophie'd caught chicken-pox from her brother, and for some reason, she had it particularly badly. She had a temperature, she couldn't eat, she couldn't sleep, it hurt her to be cuddled, but all the same she wanted cuddling. She was really sorry for herself—and you can't tell a little scrap like that not to worry, she'll be better in a week. Doesn't mean a thing. . . . After three days and nights of this, my wife was completely exhausted. If I could have just had a morning or an afternoon at home I could have helped. I mentioned it to the great man, but no response. I think he'd forgotten what it was like to have a sick child at home. Or perhaps he was never bothered about that sort of thing. At any rate he obviously thought Service business was more important. But I started thinking "Is it? Is it more important to me?"

Actually, I went back to my desk and sorted through the "In" tray. Less than half of the stuff was what I'd call important—directly related to defence—most of it was, I don't know, "oiling the wheels", "showing the flag", "talks about talks", tremendously time-consuming and some of it unbelievably trivial. I was furious. I wish I could say I went straight back and repeated my request more forcefully—but—I didn't.'

It is frequently argued, with some justification, that men employed in a whole range of civilian occupations have to devote themselves similarly to their work. They too, have to demonstrate their loyalty by uncomplainingly working extra hours, attending social functions and keeping family life separate and even subordinate to work demands. In fact, it would be hard to think of an occupation which *never* made demands beyond the call of duty or the letter of the contract. The difference, however, lies in the fact that in civilian life, the duty to do one's job competently is seen distinctly from the desirability of doing it fully and well, by meeting the wider obligations which the job may carry with it. For example, a garage mechanic would be expected to turn out early on a snowy day to undertake an urgent vehicle recovery or repair job. If he were late, or reluctant, or lazy, it would not go down well with his employer, but if, having done a good job, at the end of the day he declined to stop off at the local pub with the other mechanics it would make not a jot of difference to the employer's opinion of the man's commitment to garage work.

Similarly, a teacher who is always ready to plan educational trips, take extra-curricula activities, referee the football, produce the play and so on, is far more likely than his less active colleague to be considered for advancement. But his colleague, if he is a sound teacher producing good results from his classwork, is not going to have his ability to *teach* called into question, only his loyalty to the school.

For military men, however, loyalty—to their Service and to the group within it to which they belong—is an inseparable part of their being considered *able* to do the job. For, in the last resort, they must be loyal to the point of death. Therefore loyalty to seniors, to juniors, to fellows, to the institution itself is inculcated from the moment a recruit puts on a uniform. And when these men, speaking with a corporate voice, that of, say, a ship's company, a platoon, or a Mess, ask something of an individual, it is very hard for him to refuse. It is so, even when the request is trivial because to refuse is to loosen just a little, the bonds of mutual obligation between fighting men. And it is upon the tightness of these bonds that their lives may depend on active service.

Imagine, for example, you are on foot-patrol in an ill-lit Belfast street. The man behind you, who you rely on to give you cover should you come under sniper fire, is something of an unknown quantity. For six months he has been with you, prior to coming out to Northern Ireland, but he keeps himself to himself. As soon as he's off duty he's away home. Never gives his colleagues much of a chance to draw him out, to discover what makes him tick. Is the man reliable? Will he keep his head in a crisis? It will take a crisis to find out, and in the meantime, you and the rest of the patrol are uneasy. . . . Is this over-dramatic? Not at all. Corporate loyalty is the very essence of military life and undermining it can be dangerous—for each and every separate individual. That is why military men are sometimes loyal to the point of absurdity.

Upon the shoulders of senior military commanders falls the task of ensuring that men's loyalty is not pushed too far. If they are asked time and again to perform duties which seem to them to be unimportant or unreasonable, that conflict too often with their responsibilities as husbands and fathers, then their natural, self-preserving reluctance to refuse will begin to waver. Men will opt out when not actually commanded to take part in corporate social activities, and morale will spiral downwards. It is a delicate matter of asking routinely for the possible, of building upon what men feel able to give and requiring that little bit extra only with good reason. But between the senior man near the top of the tree in his fifties and the man near the bottom in his twenties comes a barrier of changed outlook. The man at the top grew up in a society where husbands and fathers viewed their role in the family as protective and directive. They may have adored their children, have played with them when small and talked with them as they grew to adulthood. But how many would have cooked for them, washed their clothes, collected them from school, taken them to the doctor? Today's father finds none of these chores remarkable and many military fathers, like others, will do these things when they can. They become involved in the minutiae of day-to-day family life and both they and their wives feel it proper that they should be so involved.

Military men today, it seems, are not *less* committed to the military, but *more* committed to involvement in family life. The two commitments must always have clashed, but the present-day expectations of young couples in general can make military couples feel particularly hard-done-by. Looking back over the extracts from conversations recounted at the beginning of the chapter, several of the incidents would probably not have appeared problematical to couples only thirty years ago—when the 'top brass' were young. Take the man who was 'two hundred miles away, playing squash' when his son was born. Thirty years ago, men were not permitted to attend births in hospital, and not every husband paced the corridors, especially if the birth occurred during daylight hours. This wife would in those days have been no different from many of the other women in the ward. Take the father who missed his daughter's school concert in the aftermath of a rugby match. As has been previously mentioned, in the past, scarcely a father was to be seen at a primary school, that was mother's province. Take the couple who had to spend money on a social occasion when their daughter dearly wanted to have riding lessons. Thirty years ago, officers were relatively better off. This is partly due to the fact that in the past an officer would not have had a house on which large mortgage repayments were due. If he were not already an outright property owner, a house would be purchased with his gratuity when he left the Service. He would almost certainly have been able to afford the riding lessons—if not a horse. Take the matter of the holiday: thirty years ago, 'ordinary' people didn't go on sunshine packages to Spain: ordinary fathers didn't take mornings or afternoons off work to help nurse a sick child. But now they *do*, and the military man is left to feel unsure about just what he can reasonably ask for, while his family too often believes that neither he nor his Service really cares what they think or how they feel.

*   *   *

Constant Adjustment to Loss and Change

Loss is the price that is paid for attachment: attachment to people, to places, to a lifestyle, even to tiresome but familiar routine. If we did not become attached so readily, loss would not be the painful and disruptive experience it so frequently is, but it is the number and nature of our attachments that give us our identity. They make us sure of our place in our corner of the world and of our value to the social groups of which we are members. Taking the transcript of almost any interview, it is quickly possible to construct the beginnings of a picture of the interviewee's social attachments. For instance:

'I'm married to a soldier. . . . We've got two little ones. . . . I do a part-time cleaning job on camp. . . . I go to judo every week. . . . Me and my two friends go into town on the bus about every other week to do a bit of shopping. . . .'

Army wife, mother, member of a work force, member of a judo club, one of a trio of friends, regular visitor to local town . . . and so forth. Most people could list numerous social attachments which they value and which help to make them the kind of person they are, not only in other people's eyes, but also in their own estimation. If any one of these attachments falls away—perhaps one of the trio of friends moves—a loss is felt. There is some sorrow and a period when the two remaining friends feel incomplete, but adjustments are made and life continues. Or say an injury prevents attendance at the judo club for a couple of months; again there is sorrow at being unable to be part of the group, there is an emptiness in the routine of the 'judo day', there is anxiety about fitting in again after an absence. Small losses in everyday life shake our self confidence a little, but by and large we accept these things as part of life and the damage to our self-esteem is rapidly repaired, time and previous experience being major factors in this process.

But sometimes repair is not so easy. It is hard when the loss has been a major one; it is hard when many small losses occur at once. Both these situations arise in the normal course of events for military wives—over and above the kind of ill-fortune which can strike any family, anywhere. The term 'wives' is used rather than 'couples' because despite the unpredictability of military life, Servicemen have the anchor of their jobs to give them a considerable degree of continuity throughout their careers, but wives and children do not enjoy this. In consequence, a cluster of problems arises associated first, with moving home—many times—and the multiple losses felt by a family when this happens, and secondly, with the absence of the husband/father on unaccompanied tours of duty or detachments. This presents a major loss to the family and requires the wife to adapt to being effectively a single parent—only to loose this position on her husband's return.

Moving House

Mary Parker is an officer's wife, now in her early forties. She describes a very difficult family move, made about five years ago at an unwelcome time, to an unwelcome place. Unwelcome, that is, as far as Mary and the children were concerned:

'Alan was quite pleased with the posting. He was at MOD [London] and it entailed an awful lot of commuting—after two and a half years, he was ready for a change. I wasn't though. . . .

We were living in a married quarter in suburban London—nice house, right near the shops, not far from the tube, a good primary school on the doorstep . . . and opportunities to make civilian friends as well as Service ones. I was incredibly busy. Ben, our youngest, started school there and I took a part-time book-selling job. . . . We joined the local church and I was on the school Parent/ Teacher Association Committee. Shortly before we moved, I was approached about being a Local Councillor—by someone who didn't know how often we had to move—of course, it was out of the question. . . .

. . . The children were nicely settled. Hannah [the eldest] had two years of excellent primary schooling and then sat the entrance exam for her present [boarding] school—passed with flying colours. . . . Rachel came on well too; she's never been quite so academic, but she was able to have ballet lessons and piano—it was all so close, and the teaching was first class. . . .

Then one morning Alan phoned me from the office to tell me he was posted. He said: "We're moving to the country!"—and he went into great detail about the job he was going to do, and I didn't say anything. I couldn't think what to say. I absolutely didn't want to move. We were comfortable, everything was ticking over nicely—and then the bombshell. Well, not a bombshell, it's unfair to call it that, he was due for a move, but I think I'd put it to the back of my mind. . . .

. . . We only had two months' notice, and we were off. And I must say it was pretty horrid. We were two thirds of the way through the tour before I even started to look on the place as home—even thinking about it brings back very mixed feelings. . . . We had super neighbours and Alan enjoyed the work—but there wasn't a civilian community to speak of, not nearby. I had to take Rachel miles for her piano, and she gave up ballet. And the school was nothing like as good. . . . Surprisingly, Ben had a lot of trouble settling down—he was very withdrawn—for a long time he didn't have any friends. . . . Rachel was just about OK but they didn't encourage her to work and she only made it to Hannah's school by a hair's breadth. . . .

. . . I didn't work there. There was nowhere to work. . . . And I had gynae. problems. . . . I was fearfully depressed—if you'd have seen me then, you wouldn't have believed I was the same person who was asked to think about being a Local Councillor. . . .'

After five years, Mary still has no difficulty in vividly recalling her grief at the time of the move. The word 'grief' is used to describe the sense of desolation following a personal loss. From bereavement, the most severe, permanent loss at one end of the scale to smaller losses at the other, such as a child leaving home or retirement from work, all losses have the effect of diminishing the sufferer, of making him or her feel less than whole.

Mary Parker temporarily lost her self-confidence. In time, she did come to terms with the new location, though she never came to love it. It was by no means her first move, neither was it her last, but it was the first she had made since returning to the world of employment and being able to take part in community activities as her children needed less supervision. Thus, having found a new set of roles for herself to replace that of 'full time mother', she lost them all in the move to a remote station. . . .

It is perhaps now easier to understand how a woman who has had difficulty in adjusting to a move (and most military wives can name at least one or two painful moves) can be badly shaken indeed should an extra burden suddenly be placed upon her. But military families suffer from unexpected sorrows like any others. A serious illness, the birth of a handicapped child, a teenager in trouble, a problem such as this occurring hard on the heels of a difficult move, can be just too much to cope with and a woman may 'go to pieces'. She may find it impossible to think clearly about even trivial matters and seek help for the most minor of difficulties for quite a long time. The helpers do not always understand. A GP whose practice includes a number of military dependants on a married quarters site is not alone in her perception of the women as a group:

'The wives are a neurotic lot. At the moment, it's back problems—one has them, they all do. I think they have too much done for them. They live in good houses at next to no rent, everything's laid on for them, so much so, they think the world owes them a living. At the first sign of trouble they expect me to mobilise the entire resources of the National Health Service—and every other government department besides!'

A solicitor in practice near a military establishment: *'In comparison with many of our clients, these people are not poor, they're not noticeably deprived, and there's not all that many of them but they do seem to generate a disproportionate amount of work—matrimonial work mostly. I don't know why this should be. . . .'*

* * *

Absent Husbands

All military men are liable to be sent away from home, without warning, to virtually any part of the world, for any length of time. But it is the men of the Royal Navy who face the longest and most regular separations from their families while serving on board ship. The BBC has in recent years broadcast two popular TV documentary series, *Sailor* and *Submarine* which looked at the lives of men who work in ships of war. Both touched briefly on the subject of the wives and families left at home, but there was no sustained following of their (admittedly, often humdrum) lives while their menfolk were away. If they had done so, they could have monitored the difficult process of adjustment to the temporary but repeated loss of their husbands.

A group of Naval wives discussed the issue. Their husbands' ranks ranged from Leading Seaman to Commander and their ages from early twenties to mid-forties, but from this apparently mixed group, ideas and feelings about their recurring loss were remarkably similar. They talked about 'phases' in the adjustment process which actually reflected quite well the conclusions of people who have researched reactions to grief. Writers such as John Bowlby, Colin Murray Parkes and Lydia Rapoport (see section headed 'Recommended for Further Reading') point out that there are various stages through which individuals pass when experiencing and adjusting to loss. Broadly speaking, they encompass the following reactions: firstly, a *numbness* at the point of loss and shortly after, when everyday chores are accomplished unthinkingly and the event is partially blocked by the mind, allowing reality to penetrate gradually. This usually leads into a period of *grief*—strong emotions of unhappiness, notably sorrow and anger which alternate with feelings of helplessness and apathy. Once the pain of loss has become less pervasive, *acceptance* of the new situation is possible and the future is faced with a greater sense of calm. The final stage is that of *rebuilding* a disrupted life; not something which can be achieved overnight, but a task which can be accomplished once the loss has been accepted and the loser's outlook has changed from negative to positive. It may be helpful to bear these observations in mind. . . .

Parting

'*The day he reports back to the ship I'm OK. Sometimes I have a weep the night before, but not on the day. I go through things automatically—you do, don't you?—the goodbyes and all that . . .*'

'*That's right. And the longer the sea time ahead, the less you have to say to each other before you part. You're both steeling yourselves, and if it's going to be a very long time, what* can *you say? I mean, when he's only off for a week or two he might say, "Don't forget to pay the phone bill" or "Try and visit grandma"—but when he's not coming back for months you both know it'll all be down to you, and he won't be around to worry about the little things. He has to forget his family responsibilities—well, to a degree. . . . He has to trust you to get on with it. . . . Saying goodbye is not as emotional as you'd expect—in the early days there were a few tears, but over the years you learn to switch off gradually . . .*'

Missing Him

'*It's that evening it hits me . . . when he's not there—*'

'*It's two or three days later—*'

'*I carry on for about a week, keeping myself really busy, but eventually I get tired and then I miss him badly. . . .*'

'*. . . The first little thing that goes wrong, I'm really angry because he's not there to sort it out . . .*'

Whether the marriage is good or poor, the man's presence is missed. The couple may have quarrelled remorselessly, or may hardly have exchanged a remark all day, but the pattern of the relationship, whatever its quality, has been broken. The sadness that a woman (or child) feels on facing this does depend on how fond the family is of one another, but it depends too on how much they have become accustomed to relying on one another. Most married couples complement each other in some ways—temperamentally, practically, intellectually, emotionally—and it would be unusual for there to be no dependence, husband upon wife or vice versa. For example, one partner tends to be the more frequent decision-maker, one partner will be the main organiser, letter writer and so on, one will more readily take the role of stabiliser and comforter while the other drives the family forward. This interdependence is the main purpose of companionate marriage. In the military situation, however, it is the independently-minded wife who copes best with her husband's absences and feels less acute sorrow when he leaves for prolonged periods. She is the one who is better able to accept life on her own or as a single parent and is confident in her own abilities as head of the household.

Coming to Terms

'*When he first goes, I worry about all the things that* might *happen . . . but once I've managed to get through the first crisis, I know I'm all right.*'

'*How ever long he's at sea I feel sorry for myself from time to time, but from Day One I know I'm in charge and I make all the decisions.*'

'*I'm apt to be—wobbly, up to the half way mark. A problem I haven't met before can throw me . . . like the gas boiler going out and not being able to relight it. I can get myself into a right stew. But there's something psychologically important about being half way through. After that it's easy. Once I'm on the downward slope I feel I could tackle anything. I even rather enjoy "single" life when I can see an end to it! I have a huge burst of energy and do all the chores we've been talking about for months. . . . By the time he comes home I'm quite smug about how well I've managed. . . . I don't let on about the difficult bits!*'

Taking Control

Some wives find it very hard to shoulder the responsibility of managing a household on their own. Some cannot, some will not cope and lurch from one crisis to another seeking support from anyone willing and able to give it. Most Families and Welfare Officers have amongst their clients a few wives like this, who need a great deal of reassurance when their husbands are away. But an overwhelming majority of women surmount their difficulties by themselves, and whilst it is wrong to say that the more frequent the absences the easier they become, it is true that a wife does develop her own coping strategies which enable her to incorporate periods of separation from her husband into her life, relatively smoothly.

'*I have two different types of existence, one when my husband's at home and one when he's at sea. . . . When he's at home, you would call me a conventional sort—I leave most of the decisions to him, I don't go out on my own socially, we*' *spend quite a bit of our time working on our house and our garden—it's an old place we're doing up. When he goes. ... I change gear. I become a different person—not suddenly overnight, of course ... I go out much more—to friends and clubs and things like that. And I become quite a strong person. I know when I've been on my own too long—my sister tells me I'm getting "strident and aggressive". She says I need toning down. ...'*

One way or another, wives find ways of restructuring their lives during their husband's absences—only to find that when their husbands return, they are the ones who must change again.

Reintegration

In looking at 'the Depot Community' in Chapter Four, the difficulty was mentioned of the man's reintegration into his family after a significant absence. If he is to preserve a viable role in his household, he has to take back his share of the day-to-day family decision-making, and whilst most wives understand this, the actual process of partial 'transfer of power' is rarely smooth.

'We always have problems with the boys.' (This Lieutenant's wife has three teenaged sons.) *'When he's at sea, I say what they can and can't do, if they want to go to a party or a disco or stay with a friend, I'm the person they have to negotiate with. ... I know pretty well what freedom they can handle and I don't let them have their heads. But when Phil [husband] comes home he thinks he should be the one to decide—and the trouble is, he gets out of touch. ... He doesn't realise how fast the boys grow up—even six months make a big difference with an adolescent. He doesn't credit them with any sense, and that's particularly hard to swallow for the eldest, because in a way, he's the "man of the family" when his dad's not around. In any case, I can guarantee that within a week of Phil coming home there'll be an almighty bust-up between him and the boys—with me in the middle. If it didn't happen so regularly I'd think the world was coming to an end, but as it is, I know its an "Event" and we just have to go through it. ...'*

Having talked about stages in adjustment to loss, a cycle of readjustment to the original married life style can also be seen. This begins with the homecoming; usually joyful, sometimes emotional, always charged with underlying apprehension. And there is also some shyness, some reserve. Despite all the macho talk about what they will do with, or to, their women when they get home, for more than a few, the first days or even weeks bring sexual problems.

Judging from conversations with wives, it is very common for women to show initial reluctance to having intercourse—a reaction which can hurt or anger the returning husband. He may call his wife frigid when, more often or not, she is shy or even afraid of his advances. She may feel them an assault on her privacy, and also on her ascendancy in the household. She may find it impossible at first to rekindle feelings of desire for a man who (albeit not entirely of his own free will) in practical terms deserted her and their children, who was not there when things went wrong and was no comfort on dark days. Love and sexual desire cannot be reconstituted like instant coffee, they need time to re-establish themselves and grow.

Similarly, for the husband, it is not unusual for temporary impotence to strike. For weeks or months his conversation in all-male company has been peppered with sexual innuendo, sexual jokes and sexual boasting. From every communal workroom and resting-place pin-ups of nude women gaze at him and heaps of dog-eared magazines feed him as much soft (and not-so-soft) porn as he wishes to consume. The macho idea of dominating sex, of *taking* and bedding a woman, by force if necessary, of seeking a female who is as insatiable as he feels, does not (in most cases) accord with the wife he has left behind. Even so, coming home, expectations are high. As the day approaches, the subject of sex will have assumed an almost overwhelming importance. But what will not have been discussed in the crew-room or the Mess will be the need for gentleness, the possibility of being patient and acknowledgement of the fact that enjoyable sex is a two-way process. More frequently than many would admit, the returning male with his urgent sexual demands finds himself impotent. A Marriage Guidance Counsellor who has worked with both Army and Navy personnel: '*For most men it is just an unkind quirk of nature—sudden self-doubt or an unwilling partner will upset them. ... More serious I think, are the men who get accustomed to "girlie" magazine fantasies, or to prostitutes ... and find it difficult to take the initiative when they arrive home to an anxious, tentative wife.*'

As both partners struggle to create a small space for themselves to begin the psychological readjustment to being together again, arguments, sulking and depression can occur. This is caused in part through each party's expectations of the reunion—viewed with the aid of rose-coloured spectacles. ... He was going to cuddle the baby, play hide-and-seek with the eight-year-old, converse warmly and unpatronisingly with the teenager. He was going to bring flowers and presents, he was going to laugh a lot and hold hands and take pleasure in simply being at home. ... Instead, he is distant with the baby and holds him insecurely so that he cries. The eight-year-old will not speak to his father, let alone play games with him, while father will not accept on anything close to adult terms, the upstart teenager—especially if it is a usurping elder son. He does not bring flowers, but bottles of duty-free whisky which his wife does not drink and says that in—wherever it was from whence he returns—there was really nothing worth buying. And instead of the laughter and the warm reassurance of ordinary, conventional physical contact, there is the urgent, untimely sexual groping as soon as circumstances permit. The family recoils instinctively from the intruder, but guiltily feeling that they should not be doing so. Father, for his part, cannot understand his children's truculence, or his

CHAPTER 7

Breaking Point

This chapter is concerned with what happens when a man finds it impossible to reconcile the two roles of military man and family man. However, it would be misleading to imply that the twin responsibilities are by nature, quite irreconcilable, or that countless numbers of military marriages are not successful. Talking to couples who had been married for more than fifteen years—and had stayed with the military—three factors emerged sufficiently often to identify them as predisposing factors for 'success'.

The first was a strong social life within the military community—couples whose many friends and acquaintances were drawn almost exclusively from military circles. They tended to be people who had not bought, or at least, had not lived in, their own houses, and incidentally, many of these mentioned their satisfaction with 'married patch' life as a reason for not buying. Such couples have a powerful, shared investment in maintaining their way of life, but figures indicate that fewer people nowadays spend years and years in married quarters, and as a consequence it seems likely that the 'social factor' will be less influential in the future.

The second factor may be more important in years to come, and that was shared professional interests. This was very obvious in some cases, such as the Padre married to a social worker, the Education Officer married to a teacher, the doctor married to a nurse, the RAF officer married to an ex-WRAF officer who had recently re-entered the Service. But there were also several examples of wives who, over the years had built up business interests of their own (a boutique owner, an interior designer, a market trader, a provider of specialist cleaning services to a large married quarter estate, to name a few) in which their husbands had invested time and money, too.

The third factor was the most common, though doubtless associated with a vanishing breed—the personally unambitious wife, who was content to support her husband domestically and socially and to take her status from him. In the forty-plus age group, women with this kind of traditionalist outlook were not hard to find; they came from a variety of social backgrounds and were of widely differing intellectual abilities. They had never anticipated carving out a career for themselves and in many instances identified strongly with their husband's career. One or two seemed almost to be 'the power behind the throne' whilst others were clearly keen to achieve upward social mobility through their husband's advancement. There is no doubt that many wives derive a good deal of satisfaction from a traditionalist role, and equally that many men's careers have been furthered by wives committed to this aim. In younger age groups, there were fewer women who seemed to subscribe to this view of marriage—and amongst the wives of the young 'high flyers' interviewed, there was really no one. . . .

*   *   *

Within a Hair's Breadth

Two years ago, thirty-seven year old Peter Lewis faced the prospect of the dissolution of his marriage and the crumbling of his career through an alcohol problem that was worsening, unchecked by colluding friends; and yet, today, he is still married to his wife, Hilary, and remains an NCO in the military. It is certain that many, many Service marriages reach this low point or one very like it, and therefore it is important to say something about the relationships which come within a hair's breadth of breaking-point—and do not break.

Peter is reluctant to discuss the past, believing it is better to leave painful memories alone and concentrate on the present. But Hilary feels that their story is far from unusual and knows other people who have had similar experiences. . . .

'*In the beginning*', she says '*it was just the drink. He used to go out two or three times a week with his mates and come back rolling drunk. Saturday lunchtimes was worst, because then the girls* [Katie aged ten and Jessica nine] *were about and I didn't like them seeing their father in that state.*' She and Peter had rows, but his behaviour seemed no worse than many other men's and the military appeared to positively encourage the image of the drinking, fighting tough-guy. It was a long time before she began to realise her husband was dependent on alcohol—and by then she felt powerless to change the situation. Any attempt to broach the subject with him brought a tirade of angry denials, and a tentative approach to one of his friends caused a 'closing of the ranks' which led to her being seen as a nagging wife. Rightly or wrongly, she felt there was no one in the military community who would be on her side and became convinced that the only hope for the family was for Peter to leave. And then she did become a nagging, whining wife, hoping to '*drive him away*'.

'*I remember the first time he hit me, but I don't remember now what led up to it. He punched me in the stomach—I was sick.*' In the morning, when he was sober, he was appalled at what he had done; but he did it again—more times than Hilary likes to remember.

'*When he turned on Katie one night, that's when we got out. He thought . . . well he got it into his head we were all ganging up on him . . . and instead of going for me, he went for Katie. . . . The girls and I* walked *into town* [a considerable distance] *and the Police directed us to the Women's Refuge.*'

Hilary started divorce proceedings, but . . . '*When we met to discuss practicalities, you know, possessions and what not . . . he was 'on the wagon' and I thought then: if he keeps this up, we could start again. . . . But I insisted . . . I wasn't going back on camp again for* anything. . . .'

The family moved into a small house, privately rented from another Serviceman, to try and work things out—and, against the odds, they succeeded. Peter is now strictly teetotal and observes with a touch of regret that this cuts him off from old friends and drinking partners, but he adds '*I've made other friends and I think I've still got promotion prospects. . . . When I was drinking, I was always thinking about leaving Hilary . . . even ending it all . . . but now—never.*'

A serious if not uncommon case-history, and one in which the husband had to change his attitude and behaviour in order to save his marriage (and probably also his career). But, equally, there are many military marriages where it has been the wife who has had to do the changing—sometimes with great reluctance.

Nigel and Lynne were in their late twenties when their marriage hit serious difficulties. Nigel was approaching the end of his engagement in the military (one which he had already extended) and he and Lynne planned to move 'back home' to Aberdeen. At that time employment prospects in the city were good and, despite the high cost of housing, they had saved enough to put a deposit on a three bedroomed semi-detached home. Furthermore, they were looking forward to their children being educated at Scottish schools—which they maintain are vastly superior to their English counterparts. Then Nigel was offered the chance to try for a commission. Lynne did not object when he entered into the selection process but says that, for some reason, she didn't think he would be successful. When he was selected for officer training, she flatly refused to go along with the idea. She couldn't see herself as an 'officer's wife', the prospect horrified her, and she felt let down after all the plans they had made in relation to the move to Aberdeen. Against this, she had to weigh Nigel's delight at his achievement and the benefits of family security and higher social status. In the end, she allowed Nigel to talk her into giving the idea a chance—though she knew that his commission would entail a further long-term commitment to the military. Privately, she resigned herself to leaving him if she continued to be unhappy, and they began to drift apart. Nigel, Lynne says, seemed ever more dedicated to his career, while Lynne quietly strengthened her own ties with family and friends in Aberdeen. She constantly made minor preparations to leave (she kept the coach timetable to Scotland in her handbag) but never quite got to the point of going.

According to Lynne, there was no dramatic 'moment of truth', her decision to stay with Nigel was made gradually. During his first posting as an officer, she found to her surprise that being an officer's wife was not as difficult or as unpleasant as she had feared. She was asked if she would help to run the base Thrift Shop, and being an organised, reliable person, made an excellent job of it. Through wives she met there, she became involved in a host of other activities, and now claims she is busier than she has ever been in her life. She is contented, for the time being at least, but is still hoping that Nigel will leave the military when the children are secondary school age. She remarks: '*We're not home and dry yet with our marriage, but then, is anybody?*'

It is impossible to know just *how* many military marriages come to within a hair's breadth of collapse and yet survive. That a great many undoubtedly do says a lot for the social and professional attractiveness of military life for those who have come to be part of it. However, there are men who find they cannot satisfactorily sustain their dual commitment to family and to Service, and have to decide between the two—though few would put it as bluntly as that.

*   *   *

The Serviceman Quits

In 1985 6,453 men left the military prematurely at their own request. This is more than in recent years, and although it does not constitute a mass exodus, any unnecessary loss of trained personnel is a drain on the national economy, requiring as it does the expensive training of manpower replacements.

Ask these men why they are leaving and they will give what they judge to be an 'acceptable' answer. Dissatisfaction with promotion prospects in general and individual career frustrations (for example, failure to be selected for a particular specialism or post) are common reasons given. Better job offers outside the military feature prominently, too, though, interestingly, many men who find civilian work before leaving accept a reduction in earnings. Family issues are seldom mentioned as an important reason for quitting—and yet, if one asks a man planning to go whether there is a family factor involved somewhere in his decision, the answer is invariably in the affirmative. It is possible to speculate why so few men cite this factor unless directly asked: it could be that the masculine, bachelor-group loyalty mitigates against a man's admitting to yield to pressure from outside the group—and from women and children at that. To do so might undermine the group, the group that must at all costs be strong. And so other, valid and truthful reasons are given, and the family influence, perceived as threatening to the cohesion of military society, is pushed into the background.

Nevertheless there are men who will concede (in private at least) that they are quitting because the demands of family and military life have become, for them, incompatible. Visiting various military bases, it is not difficult to find men who are considering leaving the Services. It is harder to find men who have actually applied to do so. They tend to be somewhat secretive about their plans until they are reasonably sure that the military will release them and that their future is as secure as it can be, in civilian life. Clearly, it is unwise for a Serviceman to *apply* to leave if there is a possibility that he could change his mind if he fails to find suitable alternative employment. Likewise, it is foolish for a man to make too much of leaving plans too far in advance of a possible exit date. In either instance, the man, if he stays on in the military, has to serve against a background of public knowledge that he is 'uncommitted' or at least, that his commitment is suspect. This does nothing for promotion prospects and does not enhance the likelihood of his obtaining interesting, sought-after posts for the remainder of his service. Although his colleagues would not intentionally behave differently towards him (most would themselves have thought about leaving at one time or another), they would in practice regard him in a different way once his application for release was common knowledge.

For these reasons, Servicemen and their families are often reluctant to talk about their decision until it is virtually a *fait accompli*. It is sometimes more useful to discuss reasons for leaving with men who have already made the move and have established themselves in civilian life. In many instances they are better able to put the decision into perspective and to review the relative importance of family circumstances at the time. The main drawback, however, in seeking out families who have settled into civilian life is that it is principally those people for whom the break has been successful who are happy to talk about it. It should not be forgotten that a significant number of men every year apply to rejoin the military, having found that 'civvy street' has problems of its own.

In talking to family men about leaving the Services, it becomes evident that they can be divided into three catagories: *potential leavers* (a large category of men 'in the planning stage' so to speak, drawing up pros and cons and looking at various options. Experience shows that many of these men do not follow their ideas through and, in fact, remain in the Services); *leavers* (men who have already asked to leave, either on completion of a term of engagement or prematurely—in which case the amount of time a man may have to wait for release could vary from a few months to several years, depending upon his age, rank and specialism); and *civilians* (for the purposes of the exercise, men who have left the military when they could have stayed, within the last five years). Although most men had come to the point of departure for a mixture of reasons, it is notable that *every one* of the family men interviewed, when directly asked, volunteered family reasons as a contributory factor to their decision.

Children's education and well being, and wives' employment were the most frequently-mentioned family considerations in deciding to quit, but under these rather broad headings, there were as many different stories as there were leavers.

Three interviews with RAF families illustrate worries over children: the first, a handicapped daughter, the second a son whose experience of boarding school was little short of disastrous and the third a more general concern about quality of life.

Sergeant Brian Simpson and his wife Gillian have two daughters, Chrissie and Michelle, aged eleven and nine respectively. Michelle was slightly brain-damaged at birth and, as a result, has learning and behavioural difficulties. She is a slender and pretty child; lively, restless and somewhat uncoordinated in her movements. Classified as ESN (Educationally Sub-Normal), she is nevertheless one of the faster learners in this group and is particularly sensitive to the occasional bouts of teasing which the 'special class' suffer from their schoolmates. Michelle responds to other children's taunts with uncontrolled outbursts of violent temper—kicking, biting, scratching and spitting. Even so, she has always been able to attend ordinary primary schools, although changing schools on her father's posting has been highly disturbing for her (this has happened twice).

Michelle has attended her present school for eighteen months and, according to her parents, she has settled well and is at last making good educational progress. For the first time since she started school, they have begun to feel optimistic about her future. The RAF has promised Brian that they will allow him to remain where he is until Michelle completes her primary education, and he and Gillian are grateful—but they want her to stay in the same locality for her secondary schooling also, moving on with her classmates to the nearby comprehensive. The school supports them in this wish. Her teacher has said that a move would undoubtedly upset her, prejudice her growing levels of concentration and set her education back. Brian has decided that next year he will not apply to extend his RAF service as he might otherwise have done, but instead will leave. He does not believe the RAF could have done more to help; on the contrary, he thinks that as he is no longer prepared to move, he should not be *permitted* to stay. He accepts mobility as part of 'the deal' and does not wish to be party to a compromise on this issue. He has two friends, ex-Servicemen, who own small businesses in the area, and he is hoping to do '*something along the same lines*' himself.

Forty-two-year-old Flight Lieutenant Barry Carter is also planning to leave the military. He has two teenaged boys from a previous marriage which broke up when he met his present wife, Jean, and they have a ten-year-old daughter of this marriage. The Carter's eldest son, Damien, won a boarding place at an ex-Direct Grant school when he was eleven. He was happy there and achieved successes both in the classroom and on the sports field. His brother Paul, two years younger, also sat the entrance exam at eleven, but failed, and his parents decided to send him to a boarding 'prep' school in the same area, with a view to his sitting the thirteen-plus Common Entrance exam and entering his brother's school in that way. Unfortunately, Paul was not happy at the 'prep' school. Despite being of above average IQ, his exam failure seemed to convince him he was 'thick' and he appeared to give up trying. His work was poor, his turn-out, scruffy, and when he wrote or telephoned home, he seldom sounded cheerful. After two and a half terms, he ran away, arriving on his grandmother's doorstep some twenty miles distant. This caused a tremendous furore, and, in the aftermath of so much attention, he seemed to settle down. He was still tearful at the end of exeats and holidays but appeared to accept that the school was 'for the best'. And it did seem that way when, at thirteen he got a place at Damien's school, even though he was, they said, 'a marginal candidate'.

Six weeks after starting the new school he was found sobbing in the lavatories—the beginning of a near mental breakdown which kept him away from school altogether, for almost a year. In retrospect, Barry and Jean say they realise that the tough, academically competitive school, which was so good for Damien, was wrong for Paul. Paul, who never liked boarding, who was under-confident in class and who was, by dint of the school's stringent selectivity, destined to be constantly near the bottom of his year-group. To make matters worse, he was not as good at games as his brother and felt he was not as popular either. Paul is now a day pupil at a comprehensive school near his home where he is rapidly making up lost academic ground, but his parents report that he has still a long way to go in rebuilding his battered self-esteem.

The unhappy episode put Damien and Paul's younger half-sister Helen off any idea of going to boarding school herself, but she is only ten and cannot expect to complete her education without a family move—unless Barry is prepared to serve unaccompanied. This the family is unwilling to contemplate. Their troubles, they say, have pulled them closer together and it is really a family decision that Barry should leave the military. Barry is philosophical about the situation; Jean feels some bitterness—bitterness towards the RAF which she thinks is partially responsible for the problem through its policy of 'forcing' families to board their children to avoid the upheaval of repeated school changes. There is not, of course, any element of compulsion over schooling decisions, but Jean feels strongly that they were encouraged to choose unwisely in order to maximise Brian's usefulness to the Service. She finds it impossible to face their own responsibility for their decisions and the ways in which they were carried out.

Lucy, Simon and Oliver aged thirteen, twelve and seven are bright, middle-class children with no school problems at all. They talk with ease and fluency to adults and possess that superficial yet impressive self-assurance often to be found in much-travelled military children. Lucy, the eldest, has attended six different schools, Simon, five and Oliver, two, but if this has had adverse effects, it is difficult to see what they are. In short, they appear to have thriven on their gypsy-style mobility. But this phase of their lives has ended as their father, Wing Commander Patrick Bates, has left the RAF at his optional exit date, his thirty-eighth birthday. His decision was made some years earlier, in conjunction with Wendy, his wife, and although senior RAF officers tried to persuade him to remain for a full career, he was not to be persuaded. Patrick and Wendy hankered after a different lifestyle; he had contacts in the world of commerce and politics and wanted to have a shot at 'the big time' before it was too late. She wanted a house with a large garden to cultivate, animals to rear and '*a huge kitchen with an Aga*'. Both of them were emphatic that their children should *not* go to boarding school. They now have their house in the country—but within commuting distance of London—and the children have settled into local schools. So far, they have no regrets. They are quick to say that military life was exciting and varied, but declare that '*enough was enough*'. They are beginning to put down roots and are happy to be able to give their children the experience of village life while Patrick pursues a new and challenging career. The move carries an element of risk and it may be interesting to note that, in addition to his RAF gratuity, Patrick is cushioned a little by a very small private income—though it is more a psychological than a financial prop.

Wendy Bates' desire for a country lifestyle brings us to consider two further cases in which, in the first, a mother and in the second, a father, found that military life was preventing them from leading the kind of family life which they felt to be right.

Lance Corporal Ian Potter was a regular soldier until last year: now, he works for British Telecom. His wife, Janice, was never very keen on Army life. She came from a closely knit family from North-East London where her two sisters had married and settled within a bus ride's distance from their widowed mother. Married to Ian, Janice lived in a succession of different married quarters in locations ranging from Scotland to Germany—but never London. At times, Janice suffered acute attacks of homesickness, especially during her two pregnancies and when their little girls were young. As a couple they made friends and enjoyed a busy social life, but Janice was not the kind of person who made close friendships with other Army wives very readily. Consequently, when Ian was away, she became withdrawn and depressed. He did not realise the severity of

Janice's depression, quite simply because he was not there to see it. A crisis brought the situation into the open when he was absent from home on a routine detachment. Janice received a telephone call from her mother to say that her sister had been knocked down in a road accident and was in hospital. Janice and the girls took the next train to London, and for five weeks Janice ran her sister's house while she recovered. At the end of this period, however, Janice could not face going home. She had enjoyed the closeness of the wider family and had renewed old friendships with girls who still lived in the area, her daughters had gone to the local Catholic school and had fitted in well, and the three of them were happy and relaxed. The prospect of returning to an empty married quarter for several lonely weeks before Ian was due back—only, she knew, to depart again a few weeks later on an exercise—made her think hard about the kind of life she really wanted for herself and her children. She decided that, whatever the cost to her marriage, she could not go back, and felt moreover that if she did, the girls would lose the warmth and security of extended family networks which they had begun to feel part of. So Janice moved in with her mother.

Ian and Janice separated and Ian moved back into barracks. But he missed his family and was unhappy in the institutional environment in which he was obliged to live. He tried but failed to persuade Janice to rejoin him and finally he decided to leave the Army. Ian was fortunate in finding employment in London relatively easily and the family seems to have 'fallen on its feet'. But the Army is now missing one trained soldier who did not himself want to leave. . . .

Just as there have always been wives who have found military life intolerable, there have similarly always been some men who have found that the deprivation of 'normal' family life has become unacceptable to them. If attitudes on this matter—discussed in Chapter Two—remain strong in today's young entrants, the number of men taking this line might reasonably be expected to increase. At present, it seems acceptable for men to say they would like to 'spend more time with their family' but few cite this as their main reason for leaving. One who does, is RN Senior NCO John Jones.

John was married, briefly and unhappily, in his early twenties. He and his wife met, conceived a child, married, went through the trauma of miscarriage and parted in under two years. They were subsequently divorced. John lived the life of a sea-going bachelor until he was thirty-six, when he met Elaine, a divorcée herself, two years his senior, with three children. She had a comfortable home on the South coast and a wide circle of friends, and when John married her, he was able for the first time to be a family man. Not surprisingly, he felt he had lost time to make up and began to be resentful when he had to go to sea. The deciding moment came when Elaine became pregnant. He was not, after all this time, going to miss the upbringing of his only offspring. Four years ago he left the Navy, and was unemployed for a frighteningly long period of time. Then he found work in the offices of a pharmaceutical company and is now able to provide a good standard of living for Elaine, her children and their young son. Of course, it is not a 'happy ever after' story, because John has to contend with all the problems and tensions that arise from being a step-parent—compounded by the arrival of a new addition to the family. Nonetheless, he is determined to savour the role of family man which he values highly, having for so many years known only bachelorhood.

In addition to pressures which have always forced some men to look carefully at the conflicts in their own lives between career and family, a newer consideration is also making itself felt. It is (as mentioned earlier), the impact of a military way of life on a wife's career. To date, it would seem that no men actually abandon their own military careers in order to facilitate the career advancement of their wives. In any event, no leaver or potential leaver interviewed indicated that this was the case. However, quite a number of men—particularly those whose military careers were not progressing as they had hoped—were finding an incentive to look for civilian employment in the fact that their wives were professionally qualified and/or capable of a real sharing of the 'breadwinning' load. In such circumstances, there also exists a pressure to make the break while the wife is still young enough to re-enter or continue employment without undue difficulty. . . .

Douglas Campbell joined the Navy as a midshipman Cadet, straight from school. Wanting to follow his successful father into a naval career, it came as a shock to discover that he was colour-blind and therefore could not be a Seaman Officer. Nevertheless, he entered as an administrator, went to sea, and thoroughly enjoyed his chosen occupation. He married Celia in his early thirties (the daughter of long-standing family friends) and they bought a cottage in an attractive Hampshire village and produced two children. At this point, Douglas began to think hard about his career. As an administrator his chances of rising to high rank were limited, however able an officer he might be. Although he considered himself able, he had to face the fact that, as a single man, his devil-may-care attitude had frequently landed him in trouble. Turning over a new leaf, though a step in the right direction, would not quickly put him back in contention for rapid promotion against more consistently conscientious fellow officers. Both he and Celia, coming from fairly affluent families, aspired to a standard of living that could certainly not be afforded on anything less than a Commander's pay. Being realistic, Douglas felt that the chances of his achieving this rank were less than fifty-fifty. Celia, before starting a family, had worked in the world of antiques and fine arts and still had many contacts in the field, and it was this which prompted the couple to start their own business.

Douglas left the Navy to set up an Antique business. It is too early to know how profitable the enterprise will be, but the Campbells maintain that Douglas's administrative expertise, allied to Celia's more specialist knowledge, should give them a fighting chance of survival—and, they hope, the equivalent of a Commander's salary within four years.

Ken Baxter is a Squadron Leader in his late thirties who is considering leaving the RAF. Lately, he completed a military Staff College course and fully expected to take up a command post directly afterwards. When this did not materialise, he began to worry about his prospects. A relatively ambitious man, keen to perform one of the key jobs in his specialisation, his failure to obtain such a job when others on the same course were successful, was a blow both to his pride and to his hopes.

His wife Pat is a teacher, whose career has been fragmented to say the least. Where Ken completed a full tour of duty in one place she was able to rise to positions of responsibility—only to return to supply work on moving house. When their children were young she accepted this, but as she approaches the age of forty and her children grow up, she feels it is 'now or never' if she is to prove herself in her own profession. Ken has not yet requested premature voluntary retirement; he is looking for alternative employment, but knows that in his branch, he will not be released immediately. Pat, meanwhile, has been appointed to a permanent teaching post.

Mick Appleton's girl-friend is a barmaid. After three years in the job— *'there's not a lot she doesn't know when it comes to running a pub'*. And that is precisely what Mick and Sandra intend to do when he leaves the Royal Marines in two years time. Their plans in respect of possible marriage and perhaps children are vague, but they have already started writing to breweries and considering what type of market they would be aiming at. Failure to achieve their goal does not seem to have crossed their minds, but Sandra has said that she won't marry Mick if he stays in the Marines.

The cost to the taxpayer of replacing Servicemen who quit is very high, and no amount of money can buy their lost expertise. Obviously, it is not advantageous to any organisation to keep within it people who would rather not belong. Furthermore, some turnover of personnel is essential if an organisation is to avoid becoming stale and resistant to new ideas. It must be acknowledged that a fair percentage of military leavers are men of only moderate ability whose replacement, if costly, is not too damaging to the military. However, a small number who leave are men of great talent (Patrick Bates, for instance) who would shine in probably any walk of life. Organisations do not need a large number of exceptional individuals—'too many Chiefs and not enough Indians' being a poor basis on which to function—but in life-or-death situations such as those found on active service, the quality of intelligence and leadership of the Chiefs, determine the survival and effectiveness of their Indians. As military historians will point out, decision-making under combat conditions is no easy task, and the man with a knack for getting things right under presure, is worth his weight in gold. Unfortunately for the military, it is other potential employers who have the gold, and too often, it is the 'high flyer' who has the ability and self-confidence to change careers. Retaining the brightest and best is not always possible, not, in every case, desirable, but the loss of such men cannot be viewed with complacency.

*   *   *

Divorce

Around one in three marriages in Britain today ends in divorce. Many military marriages—and remarriages—suffer this fate. Causes of marital breakdown are invariably complex and any marriage is subject to all manner of strains and tensions. Within the military context, however, there are some situations that seem to crop up very frequently. Here, the contingencies of military life are certainly a causal element in marital breakdown. Four such situations are considered in this section.

It will probably come as no surprise that the first situation to be considered is the involuntary separation of young couples before their marriage has had time to 'gel'. A young husband is sent away on detachment or posting, both partners are lonely and infidelity on the part of one or both of them leads to divorce. The Army, with its large number of early marriages, is especially conscious of this problem. A video designed for chaplains to show and discuss with young soldiers and their girlfriends was made by the Army and catalogues many of the pitfalls that exist for couples beginning a marriage against a background of military life. Entitled *For Better, For Worse*, it starts with the wedding of a young soldier and his attractive teenaged bride. The couple's hopes are high and they are obviously very much in love, but it is equally obvious that they have not begun to imagine what their day-to-day life will be like after marriage. The husband knows he is to be posted to Germany and that his wife will be able to join him there; they are excited at the prospect of setting up their own home. In the event, the wait for a married quarter is short and the film shows the pair reunited in Germany, where they set off to view their new home. . . .

An estate of drab blocks of flats, some way from the nearest town; washing flaps in the wind, small children play. . . . Inside, the flats are adequate, if cramped, but the walls are paper-thin and any raising of voices can be heard by neighbours. The young wife has to make her home here as best she can, without the aid of her own family and friends who seem a world away, back in England. Her husband, accustomed to the military environment, fails to notice how bewildered she is and makes her loneliness worse by spending time in the evenings drinking with bachelor friends. A corporal's wife tries to be friendly, but before the girl has a chance to find her feet, her husband is sent on a four month detachment to Northern Ireland. Soon after he leaves, she meets another young soldier. He is kind, she is attracted to him, the neighbours gossip. . . . In the film, the attraction does not lead to sexual infidelity—the point having been made, the script takes the story onwards to an unplanned first pregnancy and other marital difficulties. In 'real life' many similar stories do not move onwards, but end in infidelity, almost before they have begun.

Linda Becker, for instance, was married to Trevor, an Able Seaman. He came from her home town and they met at a disco when he was on leave. They knew each other for just over a year before they married, but for much of this time, he was away at sea. On marriage they rented a quarter on a naval estate and Linda became friendly with one or two of the wives of her husband's shipmates. During their first year of marriage, the ship undertook a long voyage which included a number of goodwill visits to European ports. Trevor's letters home were, she says, *'funny but short'* and she came to rely on her friends for news. When the ship came in, the Beckers and two other young couples went out for a meal together to celebrate, and about half way through the evening one of the husbands passed around some photos taken over the previous months. It was evident that they had enjoyed some eventful 'runs ashore'. A week in a Dutch port produced pictures of a group of sailors and a few local girls—and one sailor seemed particularly friendly with one of the girls.

'Trev was in about four photos, mostly in the background. There was one of him holding hands with this girl and some with him talking to her and one with him putting his arm round her ... I went mad.' Trevor, apparently, was amazed, and later, when Linda broached the subject again, he was annoyed and not at all remorseful, yelling:

'You married a sailor, what the hell did you expect?' She left him, moving back home to her parents. They had no children and the marriage now seems to Linda—and no doubt to her ex-husband also—to have been little more than a bitter-sweet interlude, a relationship which never took root. Older, sadder and, she hopes, wiser, she has not since remarried: *'If there's a next time, I want to be good and sure about my bloke.'*

A second period of difficulty often occurs in military marriages when a young couple starts a family. Some wives (understandably) find it hard to cope with the responsibilities of parenthood when their husbands are away on duty and they are living at a considerable distance from their families of origin. Worries about budgeting and running a house combine with loneliness and anxiety about looking after a baby. In the end they can overwhelm a young wife—some of whom simply pack up and go home to their own mothers. Again, it is young soldiers and their wives whose marriages are particularly vulnerable to the pressures of parenthood at an early age.

The marriage of twenty-year-old Private Martin Smith to his eighteen-year-old wife, Anne, ended recently in rather dramatic circumstances, but difficulties had been building up for a long time. Martin and Anne met at school in Newcastle. Martin joined the Army but maintained his friendship with Anne; they got engaged when she became pregnant and were married when their daughter Lisa was five months old. Soon afterwards, the small family was able to move into a married quarter in the south of England. Within months, Anne was expecting a second child; she was seventeen. Had Martin been a regimental soldier, it is possible that he and Anne might have been more closely supported, or, to put it another way, more closely watched, as they were clearly in a difficult position. But he was—is—a member of one of the Army's Corps, and was one of many young married men in this section of the Army. When the couple first moved on to the estate, they were visited by all the usual official, semi-official and volunteer callers and Anne was given details of all the activities which took place in the locality. She was, however, too shy to join anything on her own, and although her neighbours made an attempt to be friendly, she complained that they were nosey. As she was not a regular attender at either the ante-natal or the baby clinic, the Health Visitor suggested that she should go along to the Community House (a drop-in centre, open every day, where mothers can meet, make tea or coffee and chat while their children play). Unfortunately, Anne was offended, believing that it was only women with 'problems' who used the centre—and she didn't want to be identified with them. So she continued to be lonely, and resisted all attempts to draw her into the community. Martin, in the meantime, was involved in two military exercises which took him away from home, and Anne found her life becoming almost intolerable. She was pregnant and not looking forward to the prospect of another baby, she was isolated in the community where she lived and was far from home, she was seventeen and miserable, and Lisa, far from being good company (which she rather unreasonably expected) was demanding. She attended to her in order to stop her from crying, but as she gave Lisa no attention in the form of play, she received little positive response in return. Lisa, in fact, being understimulated, was somewhat backward for her age and this fact caused the Health Visitor to keep an eye on her. So it was, that, during the second of the exercises, the Health Visitor passed the house late in the morning and noticed that the curtains were still drawn. She called, and discovered Anne in her nightclothes; nothing had been done in the house for several days. Neither Anne nor Lisa had eaten, and Lisa was lying in her cot, dirty and literally starving. Anne was feeling physically unwell due to high blood pressure as well as being in a seriously depressed mental state. She was admitted to hospital and Lisa was taken into the care of the local authority.

The Army did respond by sending Martin home, but as far as Anne was concerned, it was too late. Her mother came down from Newcastle to visit her in hospital, and when she went back home, she took Anne—and eventually Lisa too. The Health Visitor commented: '*From the point of view of the welfare of the child and the coming baby, it was probably the best thing that could have happened, but I know the husband was very cut up about it.*'

Money problems are a source of marital friction between partners of all social classes, in all walks of life. The military marriage is not exempt from financial pressures, and though earnings are generally reasonable, the military life style itself throws up money-related difficulties with which husbands and wives have to grapple. Take, first of all, the absent husband. A man goes away, on duty, for a couple of months, perhaps longer. During that time his wife will be receiving household bills and making expenditure decisions necessary to the functioning of that household. Not all women are good managers of money and some husbands return to find their families in dire financial straits—often not just once or twice, but *every* time they go away. Not all men trust their wives with money, or feel it right to allow them access to more than a small amount. When this has been used, women may have little more than their Child Allowance to live on and be reduced to circumstances of real poverty until their husbands return. And some wives, even those who have access to a joint bank account and can manage money perfectly well, discover to their horror that their husbands spend large amounts of cash when they are away, depleting the family's resources dramatically.

Take, secondly, the social aspect of military life, an essential part of the job. It is important for a fighting team to know one another well in many moods, on and off duty, but financial provision is not made to assist this. As it stands at present, the man who joins in socially with his colleagues does so in the knowledge that the money it costs could have been spent on his wife, his children, his house. Meanwhile, the man who avoids social mixing, moves the military closer towards a 'Nine to Five and Home for Dinner' mentality—a mentality undesirable in a fighting man.

Take, thirdly, the question of debts. In today's world of hire purchase, mail order and easy credit, it is simplicity itself to accumulate hundreds of pounds worth of debts. But when the cheques begin to bounce, the military authorities are called in, and the debtor is deemed to have brought his Service into disrepute. In serious cases the man may be discharged—a factor which greatly discourages military men in financial trouble from seeking help, and keeps the burden of worry inside the family. It is no wonder that many families fail to withstand the pressure of this burden.

A case in point concerns Robin and Sheila Miller. Robin is a quiet character who married later in life than many of his fellow airmen. His ex-wife is a vivacious Irish woman, popular and attractive, and they have three daughters. From the start they lived well, and, according to Sheila, spent up to the limits of their income, never saving, never investing. Robin's promotions allowed for an increasingly comfortable life style; they led an active social life, and Sheila adored fine china, good clothes, a smart car and so on. Robin was commissioned, but once a Flight Leuitenant, opportunities for advancement in his branch were limited. He and Sheila built up an overdraft with their bank which might have induced them to pause for thought, had they not been posted to the USA. Here, not only were they able to live within their means again, but were introduced to even more expensive spending habits (such as always buying the *biggest* version of any product) which they subsequently brought back to England. And then they ran into trouble. Without the allowances that had cushioned them in the States, with expensive tastes, an acquisitive life style and a lack of foresight when it came to budgeting, they soon discovered they could not manage on Robin's RAF salary. Moreover, their daughters were no longer little girls, but demanding teenagers with a 'live now, pay later' attitude themselves— learned, no doubt, from their parents. Sheila took a part-time job in a shop, but it was not long before payments due on overdraft, bank loan and credit card debts rose to a frighteningly large proportion of their total monthly income. Robin was doing well at work, as usual, but there was no immediate prospect of promotion or of much increase in salary. He did not consider approaching anyone for advice about his financial circumstances.

At this point, fortuitously, Robin was offered a job using his technical skills in a civilian company, prepared to wait six months for him. The salary was high and there was a company car and family membership of BUPA. It seemed a heaven-sent opportunity to get back on their feet, and Robin took it. The RAF released him, and he and the family set up home as civilians.

The first problem was that they had to buy a house within reasonable distance of Robin's office—and Surrey is not a cheap area for a first-time buyer with three children. Mortgage repayments were crippling, rates, likewise, and they were living in a much smaller house than their married quarter. In addition, they both missed military life. Robin loathed the lack of variety in his new job and the need to worry endlessly about the solvency of the company. Sheila missed the closeness and gossip of the married patch and the conviviality of the parties and dinners in the Mess. Mortgage and rates arrears, telephone disconnection and repossession of stereo equipment raised tempers all round, but resolutions to curtail expenditure were short-lived. The threat of electricity disconnection was the last straw. After a furious row, Robin left, and Sheila had to pick up the pieces.

Three years on, Sheila is the first to admit that family overspending was more her fault than Robin's, but until the responsibility for controlling it was hers alone, she made little attempt to change. She now lives in much reduced circumstances, but is proud of the way in which she has coped. She still sees Robin from time to time, but they are legally separated and she, unlike him, has no wish to get back together again: '*I've grown up in the last three years and I can handle my money. With Robin I'd be back to the beginning again in no time. Its like when we go out for dinner, we have the best thing on the menu, we're no good for each other. . . . I feel sorry for him, he's come out of it all very badly. But I couldn' take him back—unless he wins the pools. . . . Not even then I don't think.*'

A fourth common cause of marital disharmony arising directly from the military way of life, occurs in well established marriages and often comes as a shock to colleagues and friends. It is disillusionment with the military life style on the part of the mature wife and mother. Over the years of marriage, she changes (as all people change) and finds herself becoming gradually disenchanted with the military and the demands that it places upon her family. Events which had once seemed so exciting—foreign travel, moving house, the hectic social round, the sudden call-out—begin to lose their charm. A weariness with it all creeps in, together with a desire which grows stronger and stronger, to put down roots, make deep and satisfying friendships and to lead a plannable, if not entirely predictable, kind of existence. Needless to say, not all older wives feel this way. Some find their enjoyment of the military life style increases as the years go by, and without questioning a very large sample, it is impossible to guess what the proportion of generally contented to generally disillusioned wives might be. But this being accepted, it is the case that this study brought to light a surprising number of women in the thirty-five to forty-five age group (notably officers' wives) who were, quite simply, fed up.

Military couples faced with this situation tend, initially at least, to attempt a compromise. Clive Bagnell is a submariner who for many years served in 'O' Boats based at Gosport. Then, on promotion, he was posted to Faslane in Scotland to serve in a nuclear submarine. He enjoys the Navy and prefers working on the nuclear vessels to his earlier experiences of cramped and smelly conditions aboard the conventional boats. Joan, his wife, and their two children somewhat reluctantly moved up to Scotland to live near the base, but they were not happy. Joan felt cut off from her own friends and relations who lived in the south of England; the children found adjustment to their new schools very difficult, with complete syllabus changes in several subjects. Although Joan did feel part of the 'submarine world' to which her husband belonged, she discovered to her dismay that she no longer cared for it. Whereas, living near Gosport there had been many other distractions, at Faslane she found the Navy dominating her whole life. Her friends, her children's friends, their conversation, their moods, everything centred on the Navy. She stayed for six months, but after only a few weeks she started to become increasingly 'anti-Navy' until it was almost an obsession. Their marriage came close to collapse as Joan insisted she *had* to get away, while Clive believed she was making an inordinate amount of fuss over temporary settling-in problems. Even-tually, it was the children's distress which convinced Clive of the serious-ness of the situation. A family argument which ended with tears revealed not only the children's school worries but also the effect which their mother's unhappiness was having on them.

Joan and the children moved back to the Portsmouth area; the marital relationship was damaged somewhat, and Joan describes their situation as 'partial separation'. Clive spends his leave with the family, but finds it impossible to look upon their present house as 'home'. He does not want to leave the Navy and neither he nor Joan want divorce, so they live a strange compromise of a marriage—not apart, not together. And other military couples are opting for the same compromise.

Maureen James is married to an Army Sergeant:

'*When the kids were little it was great. We were like a big family* [on the married patch]. *I never minded moving and I never minded the lads going away, there was always somebody to turn to. But now its not the same. I don't know whether its getting older or that times have changed . . . perhaps it's both. Now I don't find so many friends—people work, they buy houses, I mean, I had a job myself, so I can't talk—but it's not so much fun. . . . And the men seem to work much harder, they're always pushing off somewhere. . . . I started noticing it when our youngest went to school, most of the other mums had children around and I was a bit of a square peg. . . . I didn't feel I belonged in the Army any more. . . .*'

The James' marriage also came perilously close to breakdown. Like Clive, Maureen's husband found it difficult to understand his wife's change of attitude and Maureen herself found it difficult to explain. The situation resolved itself gradually. They bought a house in the vicinity of the military camp and moved in. When Maureen's husband was posted, she and the children stayed on, and although it was often difficult, he came home as frequently as possible. He is due to leave the Army soon, and Maureen is hopeful that local contacts made in the neighbourhood where she lives will help him to find employment. But living as a family again after a substantial period of 'semi-detached' marriage, she knows may prove to be no easy task. . . .

Compromise also comes in the form of wives going along with husband's wishes for one tour of duty on the understanding that he will put in a forceful request for something more congenial next time around. This *ad hoc* method of bargaining between husband and wife and husband and Service goes on all the time and those responsible for postings are generally sympathetic—within the limits of military efficiency.

There comes a point in some marriages, however, where compromise is either not working or is not possible and then either the Serviceman leaves the military, or his wife leaves him. Sally is the ex-wife of a senior RAF officer. Their marriage ended, with the decree nisi coinciding with what would have been their twentieth wedding anniversary. It began with four happy years when Sally and Ben, her husband, were part of a group of young married couples and bachelors with girlfriends, whose often riotous lives revolved around the Squadron. Sally was in employment and their income was high in relation to their needs. They were not the first in their 'set' to start a family; by the time Sally and Ben's daughter Emily was born, christenings had become a regular social event in their lives. As a housewife and mother, Sally felt that her status had diminished, the camaraderie that had existed amongst their 'set' had gone, and now they were divided in two—the young married men, and their wives with children—and Sally found that, as a mother, she liked squadron life less than she had done before.

Two children and three postings later, Ben was sent to work in a ground appointment at the Ministry of Defence in London. The family moved to suburban married quarters, and, for the first time, Sally lived according to a pattern which was familiar from her own childhood. As her father had done, Ben left the house at the same time each morning to travel to work, and at the same time each evening, he returned. Nearly every weekend he was at home, and the leave which he planned, he was able to take. Sally appreciated the choices available in Suburbia that did not exist in rural areas. There were several accessible shopping centres with many different shops, plenty of places to go for an evening out—restaurants, cinemas, theatres and so on—choices she had not realised she was missing until they were suddenly available again.

After three years, Ben was promoted and posted to a squadron overseas as a Flight Commander. He was delighted; Sally, less so. However, it was not an unhappy time. The family took advantage of their foreign location and spent as much time as possible sightseeing; the children enjoyed the experience, and Sally began an Open University course. Some 'official' work was expected of her, but on the whole, it was not arduous. She and Ben entertained a little at home, she attended station and squadron coffee mornings, she helped to organise a crèche, she became involved in the production of the station magazine, she helped to run the Wives' Club. She was content to do these things, but in no way felt that this was how she wanted to spend the rest of her life, so it was with some relief that she heard the news of Ben's next posting, to a Command Headquarters.

The family moved back to the United Kingdom, they bought a house, the elder child went to boarding school and Sally took a job that paid rather well. This tour of duty and the course which followed it saw them settle into a half-Service, half-civilian way of life during which time Sally moved into a better job, working flexi-time, and her income funded the purchase of a bigger house, closer to London. Everything was going splendidly and Ben was rewarded with promotion and a Command appointment—provided his wife would accompany him to the rural station where he would be based. Sally was frankly appalled at the prospect, but felt she owed it to Ben to acquiesce. She gave up her job, her younger child joined the elder one at boarding school near London, and she accompanied Ben fully intending to throw herself into military life.

The task proved more difficult than she had imagined. She missed her children, she missed her home and could not settle into the married quarter which felt empty and cold and she missed her job, for many reasons. She missed the intellectual stimulation which it provided, the easy friendship of colleagues, the status which she had aquired and the money which she had earned. In her view, the life of a full–time Service wife provided no compensations. Their cost of living was markedly higher than before, with official socialising to be done and a selection of evening clothes to be bought. The voluntary community work which had been an enjoyable contrast to housework and children when she was a Flight Commander's wife, neither occupied enough of her time nor engaged enough of her interest to sustain a satisfying life. Ben, meanwhile, had fitted cheerfully back into station life and assumed the mantle of command with ease. He was exceedingly busy and although he was aware of Sally's lack of enthusiasm, he claims not to have realised just how miserable she had become. He went off '. . . on a short detachment and returned, fully expecting preparations to be underway for a small dinner-party arranged some weeks earlier. He was therefore surprised and annoyed to find that the car had gone and the house was empty, but moments later his annoyance turned to dismay as the truth became evident. A note from Sally, propped up against the telephone stated simply that she was sorry, but she had made up her mind and was leaving. . . .'

Ben was bewildered, hurt and embarrassed and was convinced that Sally was neurotic and vindictive. Sally was sure Ben cared only about his career. They had stopped communicating properly some time before. Each assumed that the other was reasonably happy when they themselves were. For instance, Sally enjoyed Ben's Headquarters postings and thought that he did too, but conveniently overlooked the fact that he viewed these tours of duty not as models of how their future life might be, but as stepping-stones to a totally different way of life. When that way of life had been achieved, and Ben was given a command post, he believed that Sally would grow to enjoy her high (if reflected) status in a small society and would find outlets for her talents and energy. It did not occur to him to doubt that this would happen, and when she told him she was unhappy, he listened but did not hear. . . .

Divorce is always traumatic; it is a public acknowledgement of defeat and disappointment. For women who divorce Servicemen, the loss is two-fold, the man and the way of life. It may have been a wretched marriage and the wife may have found military life unbearable, but the absence of both leaves a large vacuum to be filled. Rebuilding a shattered life in these circumstances is not easy. Still, for some, shedding the military part of the package is a relief:

'When I married him I didn't realise I'd married the Army as well . . . by the time we split up, it was the Army I really wanted to divorce . . .' (Corporal's ex-wife.)

CHAPTER 8

The Military and its Families: Which Way Forward?

The previous chapters have set out to describe the way of life of Service families and to highlight social pressures on the military man who is also a family man. Interviews and case histories have shown some of the difficulties involved in sustaining a dual commitment to a military career and to the role of husband and father in a modern society. Well known, well documented trends—towards increased home ownership, more voluntarily unaccompanied service, increased numbers of working wives and a high divorce rate—point towards the gradual 'civilianisation' of military families which is occurring and which creates dilemmas both for the families concerned and for the military machine itself. At present, there is no doubt that the military way of life places too great a strain on too many families, and that, as a result, many good men leave. Furthermore, amongst those who stay, are a significant number who have severe family problems which require continual intervention from Service and civilian welfare agencies.

It is, of course, easy to look at any institution and spot areas where all is not well; it is less easy to identify the root cause of the malaise and very difficult indeed to suggest sensible remedies. In the case of the military, numerous small studies have been made by serving officers in recent years and none has had any difficulty in pinpointing problems regarding families and communities. Wives' careers, children's education, fewer families in married quarters and the consequent imbalance of these communities as more of the older families move out, a reluctance to go to remote locations, family pressure to quit the military mid-career ... these are some of the issues that arise time and time again. Change is obviously needed, but to date, changes that have been advocated have been relatively minor, practical matters, aimed at making life a little easier for Servicemen and their families—better house purchase schemes, nicer married quarters, reduction of unnecessary mobility and turbulence, a 'voice' for wives at Whitehall, higher salaries and so on. Most of them useful suggestions, but peripheral to the heart of the matter, for at the heart of things lies an *attitude*,[1] an *assumption* which has been part of the 'military outlook' for generations but is now anachronistic and positively damaging. This assumption is that military men, military families and military communities are 'Crown Property', set apart from the rest of society; to be cared for, managed and controlled. It is seen as being for the general good and in the interests of military efficiency—only this attitude no longer works for the good of all, neither does it promote efficiency. Change must surely proceed from an acknowledgement of the fact that military families are not helpless dependants but citizens with hopes and ideas and rights of their own, that a good many military men do not feel themselves irrevocably bound to their Service and possess highly marketable qualifications which they can take elsewhere, that military communities are no longer scattered all over the world but are predominantly here, in the United Kingdom. The military has been dismally slow to begin to adapt to these altered circumstances, but adapt it must. This chapter, with some trepidation, explores alternatives to the fundamental but outdated concept that Service personnel, families and communities are essentially *owned* by the Crown.

*　　*　　*

Starting Points

Crystal-ball gazing is a risky pastime; life has a habit of taking the most unexpected of turns and making the predictions of experts look foolish. But plans have always to be made on the basis of the 'best guess' as to future requirements, and so it is a worthwhile exercise to stand back a little and re-examine the strategic, social and economic factors that have been exerting a profound influence on the military for the last twenty years.

From a strategic point of view, gone for ever is the British Empire, and almost gone are military commitments arising from the imperial past. Here to stay is the Western Alliance of Nations, with Britain acting in collaboration with other powers as *one* of the leading military forces in Europe. The military is an arm of the state, operating against a background of peace in Europe (albeit uneasy peace at times) and nuclear deterrence. Although constantly prepared for all-out war, in practice the military role is moving closer to a 'policing' task. This is certainly a development to be welcomed, but it is a role which has its pitfalls. For policing, be it the conventional policing of civilian populations or policing which calls for the armed intervention of a military force, can only succeed where it commands a high degree of political support. Understanding such tasks, the military is, willy-nilly, involved in sensitive political issues. If military men are to perform well in these circumstances it is important that they are *not* a 'breed apart'; they must be alert and open to informed public opinion, they must truly belong to the politically fragile world which they police. An isolationist military will in future not just be less effective, but could actually be dangerous. To carry out a peacetime deterrent and policing task, the British public expects to maintain a low profile, high efficiency professional force, and governments will doubtless remain strong in their resolve strictly to control defence expenditure. This means that bright ideas to improve the lot of military families cannot cost exorbitant amounts if they are to be taken seriously. It also means that there will be an increasing need for highly skilled manpower to serve for longer periods of time in order to amortise training costs and, in consequence an ever larger proportion of career military men are likely to be family men also. Reducing the conflict between career and family should therefore be seen by the military as a singularly important issue.

Regarding social influences of recent years, it would seem that the ideal of the 'symmetrical family' is now widely accepted. Many, if not most, young fathers expect to be involved in the day-to-day running of their households and the upbringing of their children. Likewise, many young mothers expect to resume work outside the home at some stage, and children tend to be treated as young adults at quite an early age. The household no longer revolves around father—not even when he is a Service man. The military will eventually have to digest the fact that paternalism will not do. It is not enough to provide material goods and services for a man's family, to 'look after them', for, over and above the basics of life— which are guaranteed by the Welfare State—people do not all want the same things. If they are able, most will opt for the freedom to choose for themselves—how and where they will live and how they will use the time which is not required of them by their employer. A paternalistic employer, with the best will in the world, is extremely restrictive, and the military is finding that numbers of its men, and still more of their families, are growing restive.

In years to come, the British military will need to attract, and, just as important, to *keep*, able men. To achieve this, the career itself must be satisfying, the man must feel he is valued, and the way of life which he adopts must not make demands on himself or his family which will be seriously resented. The 'Crown Property' attitude which the military customarily adopts towards men, families and communities *is* resented— not bitterly, but in some quarters quite firmly—and is in small ways, being challenged. If the military does not take the bull by the horns and radically re-think its attitude, changes will occur piecemeal and not necessarily in desirable directions. Two aspects of the 'Crown Property' mentality should be appraised in the light of current circumstances: the Us and Them, Service and Civilian divide, and within the military, the Heavy Hand of Paternalism.

*   *   *

Us and Them

The British military keeps its distance from the rest of society, it is apolitical, traditionalist, self-contained. These were very important characteristics in the days of Empire, when a majority of men served overseas and had to maintain communities in far-flung foreign lands. Keeping a strong sense of identity, pride and purpose was essential, and to do this a military garrison was obliged to look inwards and draw strength from its sense of separateness. Nowadays, with the military based firmly in the UK, this 'us and them' attitude which still prevails is, at best, faintly ridiculous, and at worst, harmful to the military and the tasks it is asked to perform. In order for a society to use its Armed Forces to best advantage (whether that be to undertake a policing role, to support civilian emergency services or to go into battle), the influential members of that society must have a fair knowledge of their Forces' capabilities and resilience in human as well as material terms. They must also care about the safety and well-being of their Forces. Years of peace and the abolition of conscripted service mean that an increasing number of influential citizens have no personal experience of the military, and large numbers of the general population believe myths, stereotypes and half-truths about them. It would appear that the public is, as a rule, as comfortable with the idea of military separateness as the military itself. This hangover from the imperial past has a tenacious power. People enjoy the idea of an invincible SAS, of romantic, steely-eyed fighter pilots, of the close ties between royalty and the Senior Service, but their understanding of what the modern military is *really* like is often very hazy indeed. It saves most people from having to think too deeply about the unpleasant aspects of the job which they wish their military to be able to do, but it is not healthy.

There is, for example, a sector of the public which thinks it is interested and informed about the subject but in fact feeds on images of militaristic glamour served up to them in films, cheap paperbacks and on TV. Of course, not all material falls into this category, some of it (notably the more responsible television documentaries) is very good, if inevitably superficial, but a regrettably large amount of the more 'commercial' matter is sensationalised, biased and tasteless. It unscrupulously sacrifices truth for entertainment and lends the military a mystique which it should not possess. For war is a sickening business and to lend it an unreal, glossy image is, frankly, immoral. The Armed Forces do not seek or revel in this type of publicity and try very hard to pitch their own recruiting material more accurately. That they do not always get the balance quite right is perhaps due to the fact that they do perceive themselves as set apart from others in civilian occupations and they do play more than a little on the mystique this exclusivity engenders.

On the other hand, there is an anti-militarist sector of the public whose thinking is equally distorted. Some campaigning pacifists clearly view Servicemen as little better than thugs, itching to get their hands on weapons of destruction. Many CND members are amazed to find out that not all Servicemen are in favour of the strategic use of first-strike nuclear weapons, that some are very troubled about the whole nuclear issue and that most would thoroughly support moves towards international nuclear disarmament. For some reason, these people think that Servicemen consider themselves to have a vested interest in 'wars and rumours of wars' and actually relish the thought of fighting and killing. The truth is that no modern armed force needs reckless ruffians in its midst (complex weaponry requires a cool head to operate and sensitive political tasks call for a *controlled* use of force and the exercising of great self-discipline by men on the ground). Yet the myth persists.

In a dangerous world, where the military possesses terrible weapons, it is not comforting to consider how unrealistic are many citizens' notions about their Armed Forces. Similarly, it is, also unsettling to realise how an isolationist stance has allowed many senior military men to be appallingly politically naive. Nowadays, this cannot be tolerated; there is too much at stake.

'Us and Them': The Married Quarters

If an isolationist attitude is unhelpful to the country as a whole, it is also unhelpful to military men as individuals and, more particularly, to their families. The 'Us and Them' philosophy is most clearly manifested in respect of families by the policy of housing them all together, away from civilians, on purpose-built married quarter estates. A majority of married Servicemen live in quarters, and the military spends a great deal of money maintaining and improving the married quarter sites. The object of this expenditure is to enable the Serviceman to pursue a family life in a manner which will interfere as little as possible with his military duties. The argument runs that he can live close to his place of work, his wife and children can benefit from the use of such facilities as the military can provide for them—and in return they will be grateful and loyal to their husband or father's Service. But the truth is that today, the traditional military community often fails to fulfill its original purpose.

Earlier chapters have looked at married quarter estates from the standpoint of their inhabitants, and have mentioned the puzzlement of professionals such as doctors and solicitors at the number of problems from which the inhabitants of these apparently well-resourced communities seem to suffer. Where family malfunctioning is concerned, at the end of the line stands the local authority Probation and Social Services Departments. They are the agencies who have a statutory duty to intervene when marital breakdown leads to contested custody of children and in cases of child neglect and abuse. It is a sad truth that military estates are commonly regarded by these departments as 'black spots'.

This consideration applies not only to the sprawling estates housing very young soldiers and their families (where the Army itself anticipates difficulty) but also to smaller estates accommodating older, more highly qualified men. RAF Abingdon is a compact station in a favourable location, close to the facilities of a town, whose main function is the maintenance and repair of aircraft. A relatively large number of men employed there are technicians. In the estimation of the RAF, it is a contented community with few social problems. Yet, *even here,* a senior social worker operating in the locality of the base and who actually deals with the confidential referral of families where children are at risk, states that, per head of population: '. . . *the RAF throws up more cases and worse cases than any other part of my area.*' This is partially explained by the fact that almost *every* family on this and all military estates, has dependant children, so that even if the incidence of family malfunctioning were to be the same as that found in the community at large, there would still appear to be a proportionately higher number of Service children causing concern. But accepting this, social workers who regularly have contact with military families seem generally agreed that deficiencies within the 'married patch' communities are responsible for creating and perpetuating a large number of family troubles. The Abingdon social worker observed: '*I see the same patterns, over and over again.*'

On the married quarter estates, the shortage of mature families and the lack of extended families leads to a dearth of role models for young parents and little support for them in terms of friendly advice and practical assistance. Many children come to the attention of social services as actual or potential cases of abuse or neglect, through the sheer ignorance of their parents. A surprising number of babies and toddlers are backward because they are understimulated, and they are not stimulated because their mothers do not realise the importance of talking to them and playing with them. And there is often no one around who can show them, in an acceptable way, how to do it. Similarly, many parents are intolerant of their small children's tears and tantrums without understanding that this is perfectly normal behaviour—that before a child has developed a reasonable command of language, there are only a limited number of ways in which he can express his emotions and make his needs known. Granny close at hand or an older neighbour or sympathetic friend can, on such occasions, be a calming and educating influence; but on military estates there is a scarcity of people like this, actually living in the vicinity.

Married quarter sites house the families of a single—and singularly possessive—employer, the military. As a result, the pressure to conform to particular attitudes is strong. As has been previously mentioned, the Services encourage the 'bachelor ethos' in order to keep the ties close between its men. Unfortunately, although this may have beneficial effects for the fighting unit, it is not so good for their families. Amongst wives on the 'married patch', tolerance of husbands' heavy drinking and evening and weekend socialising with male colleagues is high. And if most of the men take it for granted that this is the way to behave, it is very hard for one or two husbands or wives to make a stand to the contrary.

A childhood spent entirely in the unstable communities of the married quarter estates can, in the opinion of many school teachers and social workers, be detrimental to children whose parents do not appreciate and compensate for the insecurity of this environment. The continual comings and goings, the difficulty of making long-term friendships and the settling in to new schools can take their toll on many children. The Child Guidance Social Worker, Peter Rayner, who for four years worked with forces families in Germany writes:[2] '*I have a steady stream of 10-year-olds who have lost interest in school and life in general. They have no special personal or family reasons to run into difficulties and would not have problems in a settled civilian or military environment. They have characteristically attended five or more schools. Their problem is that they reach an age when they have sufficient insight to conclude that there is no point in making friends or settling at school only to move on a year or so later.*' (An aside: later in the same article, which, incidentally, is not anti-military in tone, Peter Rayner remarks: '. . . *the military environment is really a sub-culture in which right-wing views of socialisation practices become the norm. . . . I have my doubts that military personnel are in fact more violent as parents.*' This to an educated readership who he believes will be of the opinion that it goes without saying that military parents *will* be more violent and authoritarian towards their children, by virtue of their membership of the military community.)

Families are encouraged to take up residence in married quarters only to find that, for many of them, the way of life is not at all satisfactory. For the communities themselves *create* many of the problems which the welfare services then have to strive to mitigate. It is not that there is *no* need for military housing any more but rather that the desirability of maintaining the type and scale of the provision that now exists, and the belief that the self-containedness of military communities, even in well-populated areas of the UK, is, of itself, a good thing, should be ruthlessly re-examined.

*   *   *

Lowering the Barriers

Advocating a dismantling of unnecessary barriers between military men and the wider society which they serve is all very well, but how is it to be done? Perhaps to begin, the military 'top brass' might consider whether the move towards the civilianisation of Service families is not, after all, a good thing, to be favoured and even assisted. Change is occurring inexorably, the question is how to work *with* it and still achieve the objective which is to run a high quality, professional military force.

From the situation we find today, the military could move away from its isolationist position by allowing development in one of three directions. The first is probably the least desirable—towards the 'Nine to Five and Home to Dinner' approach to military service currently being combatted within the American forces. This attitude could gain ground in Britain if the armed forces continue to have difficulty in holding their skilled men for as long as they would wish. If, like the United States military, they should find themselves in stiff competition with civilian employers, they could be tempted to permit their Servicemen to move towards civilianisation in order to offer congenial working conditions. But, as observed earlier, 'congenial working conditions' are not the best imaginable preparation for active service. Families could be much less mobile, wives could pursue their careers more easily and children's education could be less of a problem, but would we be better defended, or worse? In a recent book, the American writer, Franklin D. Margiotta asks: '*Is it time to investigate the concept of the 'soldier-citizen'—one who wears a uniform but shares virtually all the characteristics of his fellow-citizens?*'[3] No doubt the soldier-citizen would be a capable and contented worker; unionised—why not?—and specialised—for he would have to be if mobility were to be reduced to a minimum. But combat-ready . . .?

Far better, perhaps, to turn the concept around and, instead of civilianising soldiers, militarise more civilians. This possible path would be a modern equivalent of the pre-imperial 'citizen-militia' and would depend upon a standing force backed by a large, well-integrated reserve. A British version would be bound to differ from other modern examples of the notion, as found for instance in Switzerland or Israel. A militia could build on the existing reservist organisations, who maintain high standards and most definitely do not work on a 'Nine to Five and Home for Dinner' basis. It is conceivable that the military and its reservists could move closer together, so that men could cross the boundary in either direction with much greater ease. This would mean that an expensively trained man could be released from the military prematurely provided he became an active reservist. In this way, his skills would not be completely lost to the country. Moreover, reservists could move into full time, regular service if their particular skills were in demand.

A militia concept has a lot to recommend it, not least among its attributes being that of 'raising the consciousness' of a greater part of the civilian population with regard to their defence forces and the use to which they are put. Admittedly, unless it were to be linked into some form of conscription (a highly unlikely development in Britain), a militia system would be as

dependent upon market forces for recruitment and retention as any other—
it would not ensure a steady supply of good entrants. But it would resist the
watering down of the military role in peacetime; it would make no
concessions in terms of working practices and conditions, they would
remain tough. It is a possibility. A sensible option for a small country
expecting high levels of commitment from its servicemen but unable to
afford to train large numbers of regulars for relatively short periods of
service. However, it will probably not happen because the tradition of
professionalism and élite specialist groups is firmly entrenched in the
British military. Reservists are looked upon as enthusiastic amateurs, and
changing minds is rather more difficult than changing systems.

A more likely development would be the third possibility, which would
be for the Army and the RAF to evolve in the direction which the Navy has
already taken. That is, maintaining a highly professionalised force, serving
for much of the time unaccompanied by their families. And in accepting
that men will frequently be separated from their families, doing everything
possible to make that separation tolerable. This would involve a good deal
of subsidised travel between home and base, effective house-purchase
schemes, a high quality welfare service with considerable expertise in
helping separated families, and flexibility and tolerance from the military in
its dealings with individuals going through family difficulties. If the Army
and RAF were to follow this lead, it would also involve their abandonment
of the principle of a hierarchy of community-working wives, taking their
status from their husbands' ranks. For families remaining in married
quarters, voluntary workers would have to be sought from all levels of the
old social pyramid, and it would require a sustained effort to replace the
officer or SNCO's wife who, in the past, 'did her bit' from a sense of moral
duty, with willing volunteers from every part of the community.

Whether or not the military establishment approves, we do seem to be
moving in this direction already. Interviews with young Servicemen refute
the suggestion that the military man himself is looking for a more
comfortable existence; the profession of arms with its attendant hardships
still attracts. But families, particularly older families, are choosing a less
mobile, less segregated way of life—and this is surely an entirely healthy
development. Civilianised families would provide more Servicemen with
contact and interests in the wider society it is their job to defend. Of course,
many families would still like the option of living in married quarters, and
in remote parts of the United Kingdom and overseas, there is often no
other accommodation available. Future provision for the well-being of
these communities far as long as they are needed must be thought out, and
will be discussed at a later point.

The breaking down of the 'Us and Them' mentality is vital to a
satisfactory adaptation by the military to social, economic and strategic
changes of the last twenty years. Servicemen and their families should not

constitute a society-within-society. But the philosophy that military men and their families are *bound* to the Crown has another facet that should also be broken down. It is paternalism.

*   *   *

The Heavy Hand of Paternalism

A professional person can be said to be someone who studies and works to gain a level of knowledge and proficiency in a given field of employment that is well beyond the reach of the layman. He puts his expertise at the disposal of an employer, who, in his turn, regards the man highly and trusts his judgement. There is an assumption that the professional will, if necessary, work above and beyond the call of duty; he is no mere hireling. There is also an assumption that the employer will not ride roughshod over the wishes of this kind of employee. Career military men would like to think of themselves as professionals; they would like the status, they would like the element of consultation with the employer and their families would like their husbands and fathers to have greater personal freedom—to be *asked* to give service, to be *trusted* to give service and only in the last resort, to be commanded to obey without question. A closer approach to professional status is not just a whim to be humoured, it could be a reality, and if the best men are to be retained, it *should* be a reality—but there is a long way to go.

The military, despite its free use of the term 'professional', has not broken away from a paternalistic, public school form of organisation. (Perhaps this is not surprising since the military influenced the regime of the public schools—from whence come most senior military men.) The hierarchy is strictly delineated and people on each rung of the ladder have power over those below them. In consequence, unless a man is right at the top of the organisation, he spends most of his career in receipt of orders and instructions from above. And in the military, these orders and instructions encompass not only the work to be done, how and when to do it, but also the clothes to be worn at work, for formal occasions and also off-duty in military messes and clubs. These, and similar restrictions, a recruit accepts when he enters the military. As he gains experience and seniority, he is given more scope for personal initiative, but at no stage does he achieve much control over his own destiny. It has been said that there is *no other way* to run a successful military machine, but this is not so—as numerous armies from the past, and present-day guerrilla and resistance forces demonstrate.

Of course, a military organisation must have recourse to authoritarian methods, especially on active service, this is not in dispute; but there is enormous potential for more individual self-determination without harming the organisation in any way.

The British military obsession with order and standardisation would no doubt make it difficult for measures introducing greater personal freedom to be accepted; indeed, most suggestions are likely to be greeted with derision. Nevertheless, areas ripe for change range from strict uniform, dress and hair regulations, to assessment of performance, with its posting and promotion consequences, to a review of the rank structure and the unwieldy number of gradations which mean very little, particularly in highly specialised areas of work. In fact, the whole of Queen's Regulations could be scrutinised with a view to giving the individual as much control as possible over his own life and work.

Bearing this principle in mind, detailed proposals for specific changes could be endlessly argued, but as an example, it is suggested that men should have far greater control over their careers and that this could stem from a change to the reporting system as it applies to the career Serviceman.

Assessment of the performance of the military man at present takes the form of a sophisticated version of the school report. Once a year at least, an assessment form is raised on every man, to be completed by his immediate senior officer and commented upon by further, more senior officers. It is a most thorough report, and a great deal of effort has gone into ensuring that the system is as honest and fair as it can be. The man's abilities at his job are assessed and his attitude towards military life, his commitment and value to his unit, his appearance, his attention to detail and the extra duties which he undertakes are noted and recorded also. A well-written assessment can provide a vivid and accurate picture of how a man appears to his superiors, and on the basis of this report he may or may not be considered for particular posts or for promotion. But there is one thing missing from all this—a significant contribution from the man himself. This omission is typical of military paternalism.

Practice varies with Service, regiment or corps and also with rank but the subject of this attention is either given his report to read or is told about it during an interview. In any event, he is given some opportunity to comment and he may even seek (not normally successfully) to have changes made. However, just as a school report is not the property of the pupil but of the parent, the military assessment is relayed to its subject as information which should be useful to him (or her). Having been told more or less what his seniors think of him, and perhaps been given advice as to how he could improve, the subject is then usually left to live with the assessment until the next one comes round in a year's time.

It is propounded that the reporting chain should be extended by one contributor, the individual concerned. He should be asked to raise his own report form, and, according to existing guidelines, to assess himself as honestly as he can. Low scores in any category would be taken as a request for further help or training; high scores would automatically be read as a request to be considered for promotion. The report would then proceed up the chain as before and subsequent reporting officers would be able to amend the assessments (without erasing the original) and then make their *own* evaluations. The annual assessment interview would then become a very useful two-way exchange: the subject's senior would gain a valuable insight into the way the man sees himself and his career (and completely unrealistic self-assessments would be particularly revealing) whilst the individual concerned could ensure that his strengths were not overlooked and his suitability for advancement would at least be considered.

Likewise, in the higher ranks of the military (in both the commissioned and non-commissioned sectors), would it not be possible internally to advertise senior posts? As it is, most men know via 'the grapevine' when jobs for which they are qualified are coming up for allocation, and many make it known to their postings officers that they would like this job or detest that one. If details of forthcoming vacancies were circulated, candidates could apply and *know* they had been considered. This need not preclude 'head hunting', invitations to apply or, as a last resort, simply directing a man to take up a particular post. A system in which the initiative generally remained with the individual would surely not harm the military and would enhance the career Serviceman's feelings of personal worth and his ability to make choices. He could, for example, apply for a post he particularly wanted or a position that would involve promotion at a time when *he* felt ready for the job.

In advocating a policy of greater individual involvement in these matters, it is stressed that this should relate to men who have already served a certain length of time in the military and who are actual or potential 'career Servicemen'. Basic grade soldiers, sailors and airmen and officers on short service commissions would not come into this category.

The effect which greater career control would have on the family of the military man would be beneficial both practically and psychologically. For the family man, the practical reward of being in the driving seat where his career was concerned would be that he could plan ahead to some extent, and in closer conjunction with the needs of the rest of his household. When to volunteer for an unpopular but necessary posting, when to take that major course, when to go for a demanding job with good promotion prospects—and when not to—these could be the kind of matters on which he could take the initiative instead of having to wait to be told what had been decided for him.

Most men would choose to put a great deal of effort into the early stages of their careers. They would ask to go on courses, undertake tedious, time-consuming extra duties and go uncomplainingly wherever they were needed. Marriage would not alter this too much, but when a couple started a family, the scene might change. This stage of family life, with children under five and often no family or particularly close friends living nearby, can be very stressful, especially for the wife. Those who were able to exercise some degree of choice, would probably avoid unnecessary separations and difficult or unpopular postings at this time. There then follows a period when the children are school-aged but not yet at the critical stage of their education leading up to public examinations. This could be a highly productive stage career-wise for the husband and probably also for the wife. Child care is less intensive and well established and the adults of the family could devote more of their energies to the widening of horizons and the advancement of careers. The next phase of family life, when the children have moved into their teens, *only* affects career men, for, by this time, others have completed their terms of engagement and left. This is where the element of individual control would not be just desirable, but invaluable, since personal and family situations vary a great deal from one set of people to another. Some men have children at boarding schools and wives who enjoy moving from one location to another. Others have children at local state schools where they wish to remain to complete their education. Some wives have moved back into employment and are keen to pursue their own careers (many of which will have become lucrative and satisfying jobs which husbands, too, are anxious they should keep). Some of these men would want to try and base themselves in a particular 'home' area where their families were already settled. Older men with adult children are quite well catered for now, since either they are still 'in' the race for promotion and are willing to undertake the type of work necessary to achieve it, or they have dropped out, and mostly have found a comfortable niche for themselves from whence they can 'work the system' until they retire. They are respected for their experience and the military is usually prepared to accede to their requests. Late in the day, they have achieved a level of self-determination which could and should be extended to younger *career* men.

Leaving aside the practical advantages, psychologically, the benefits of such an attitude would perhaps be even greater. For the family man trying to run a career in the military would not have to combat the irritation, the frustration, and, on occasion, the debilitating effects of helplessness. It is acknowledged that some branches of the military are more able than others to accommodate individual career decision-making. (A regimental soldier has little choice but to go where his regiment goes—or has he? There is interchange between battalions, companies and platoons, there are courses and headquarter postings. For career men, even here there is scope for them to assume a more truly professional status in respect of the utilisation of their own skills.)

The event of greater self-determination for career men would inevitably alter their families' perception of the military at a stroke. In the final analysis, it would have control, absolute control if need be, over their husbands and fathers; but if, in practice, much of this control—in as many areas as possible—were delegated back to them, they would not feel so keenly that the men were wedded more tightly to their Service than to their wives and families.

*   *   *

Paternalism and Families

The British military holds a paternalistic view of its responsibility towards families of its personnel. It traditionally extends its care to them, and attempts to maintain control over them. Nowadays, however, the control is illusory and the care is often rejected or resented—especially when it is offered to families as though they were goods and chattels: 'Wife of —' 'Child of —'. Army and RAF wives are subjected to a certain amount of pressure to accompany their husbands from quarter to quarter, throughout their service, and to carry out unpaid community work wherever they go. This pressure can amount to outright blackmail, offering a man a command appointment but withdrawing the offer if his wife does not agree to accompany him. This kind of manoeuvre is not calculated to win the gratitude and loyalty of modern wives. Yet it remains important for the military to gain the support of wives, since it needs to retain the service of their expensively-trained husbands. So, how should it go about this task?

The first priority is to change attitudes. Paternalism has to go. Wives do not wish to be treated like children; many of them are as well or better qualified than their menfolk, and quite capable of running their own lives. The military has to accept this, and adopt a lower profile altogether. Help would often be welcomed if it were offered in a more generous, more dignified fashion.

To give examples: the entitlement to married quarters is a real godsend to many young couples, but it is a provision that causes discontent later on, as families are subjected to the unnecessary humiliation of Marching Out. The levy of a standard cleaning charge and the abolition of this ridiculous practice is long overdue. Again, the access which families have to treatment in excellent military hospitals should be a tremendous bonus for them; instead they are made aware at every opportunity that they are dependants. Their husband or father's rank and name is on their documents, and staff are made all too aware of patients' status. There is so much that is good that the military can provide for its families at every little cost to itself, but it must be sensitive to the needs of these people and must listen to what they say.

For a long time now, Army wives have, through the Federation of Army

Wives' Clubs (a respectable and conservative body which nevertheless is treated with extreme suspicion by the Establishment) asked for more consultation in policy-making which concerns families, a 'voice' at Whitehall, better house-purchase schemes, more help on moving house in respect of finding suitable employment for themselves and better information and advice regarding children's education. Their views are politely acknowledged—and nothing much happens. Progress is painfully slow because the military persists in treating families as 'Crown Property'; by the time they realise that the *goodwill* of families is vital, many more may have influenced their menfolk in the direction of premature retirement.

Paternalism and Communities: The Way Forward

Having discussed military communities in relation to the 'Us and Them' outlook of the Services, we must now ask how these communities can best be assisted in the future. If, as seems likely, the RAF and Army begin to follow the 'naval' pattern of more settled families and more unaccompanied service, what will happen to their communities? For whilst the Navy is centred on the home ports and its main concentrations of families are around the areas of Plymouth, Portsmouth and Rosyth, the other two Services are widely scattered. ... And yet, concentrations there are: the Army on Salisbury Plain together with the RAF Air Support stations of Lynham and Brize Norton account for a considerable number of Servicemen and families in one relatively small triangle of Wiltshire and Oxfordshire. East Anglia, too, is home to very many Army and RAF families—in fact concentrations of military population spring quite readily to mind once one considers the Army and the RAF together. These locations already contain many retired Servicemen and numerous families of serving military men, living in their own houses. Embryo 'depot communities', naval style, already exist, what they lack is a centre, a nucleus.

Outside the populous areas, the Army and the RAF have units stationed in remote parts of the UK and overseas. The manning of these units is crucial, but the future of the communities which they support is unclear. If the *expectation* that married men will be accompanied on such postings (where there are married quarters) is abandoned, which families would actually go? Inevitably, they would be largely the young and the inadequate. Add to this combination the isolation factor, and you have a recipe for disaster. The problem posed by the remote communities has to be faced.

In short, it seems probable that the military will have to accept that in the future, most of its families will either live in depot-type communities— many of them in their own homes—or in remote communities, and it is to the issue of how the military could usefully assist these two types of communities that we now turn.

To Serve a Depot Community

Taking the 'embryo depot communities' of Army and RAF personnel in various regions of the UK, it would not be difficult to provide good quality welfare services for all military families from a central point—probably from the largest or most accessible base in the area. A specialised team comprising for instance, health workers, housing staff, chaplains, social workers, perhaps a probation officer, certainly an education adviser, would be able to direct its chief effort into responding to the needs of families in the married quarters. Great attention could be paid to creating and assisting community projects on the estates and in involving occupants in neighbourhood schemes. But although the quarters sites would receive much attention from the welfare services—and would need it, as more families would be helped and encouraged to move into the wider community, leaving many of the young and the less able behind—these services would also be available for consultation by military families living in the region. In this way, welfare services could provide assistance to all ranks, ages and status-groups—right across the board. Centralising services in populous areas would facilitate the employment of better qualified, better trained staff, and would also create centres for the training of Servicemen to take up posts with a welfare role. (A need that is at present not being met.) At the centre, professional standards would have to be high and links with all the units in the region and all the civilian welfare agencies would have to be strong. There could be scope both for workers to be recruited from within the military and sponsored during their professional (CQSW) training and for others to be drawn directly from civilian sources. As the supervision of staff and responsibility for numerous volunteers would be part of the job, plus the organisation of in-service training for military men with welfare responsibilities, it could be a challenging field for the specialist to enter and could provide an experience of social work at several levels. Moreover, a good team could provide support, ideas, encouragement and evaluation of results for one another—things that one worker, operating at a single location , sorely misses. Communities are built on the interdependence of their members, and they are similarly best served by teams of people pooling their efforts and their ideas. Royal Navy experience of running a welfare service for a depot community has so far been encouraging: there is much that the other two Services could learn from them. . . .

To Serve a Remote Community

Remote communities are a different matter. A working definition of a remote community would be one maintaining accommodation for families that was too far away from other military establishments to join with them in sharing the services of a centralised welfare team. In such instances, although the size of the units in question would vary considerably, the self-containedness of the communities would enable a similar approach to be applied to all. The aim would be to safeguard those communities and to try and achieve a healthy cross-section of families opting to live in them.

They would have to work in a fairly traditional way; traditional, that is, in the sense that Service personnel would perform their military duties while their wives would be limited in the main, to support tasks. But if this kind of arrangement is to be sustained, a huge effort would have to go into opening up areas of work—both paid and unpaid—for wives to do. It is unrealistic nowadays to expect energetic and educated women to accompany their husbands to isolated parts of the country or to stations overseas, there to be decorative and sociable, to hold coffee mornings and dinner parties and arrange flowers ... especially if the women concerned are punctuating careers of their own to do this.

A three point programme is suggested in respect of designated remote communities. Firstly, there would be the provision of a certain amount of paid employment on base for qualified wives in their own occupational spheres. Much of this would have to be part-time work and may not fit exactly the qualification and training a woman may have had, but it should certainly be *relevant* to her career. If this were to mean the creation of part-time work for teachers or the payment of an extra doctor to do certain clinics, so be it. Unit administration would benefit from having extra workers on a 'supply' basis and the health care of the whole community could be improved with the aid of part-time workers—perhaps in the field of preventive medicine. Taking a narrow view, this sort of effort would cost valuable taxpayers' money, since many of the jobs created would be surplus to minimum requirements. But in terms of expenditure on a comparatively few 'special cases', it would be money well spent.

A second measure to widen the scope for the employment of wives would be to pay key people in community work posts. In accordance with tradition, one post could be offered automatically to the most senior officer's wife in residence, the rest could be applied for like any other job. One post might be that of coordinator for voluntary work—as voluntary work would comprise the third point of the plan.

Voluntary tasks of all shapes and sizes should be available to anyone who was interested in offering time and skills for the benefit of the community. And, as advocated earlier, work should be recognised by the giving of a reference. Of course, not all women want to work, but very many do, and just as the concept of the husband's supportive role has broadened, so also the concept of the wife's supportive role has changed. Now that wives have many skills outside the domestic sphere (and fewer within it), they wish to use their talents to help their husbands, their families and the communities in which they live. What, for example, is the point in telling an accountant she'd be welcome to serve teas at the Wives' Club (when she makes lousy tea) while she could be a superb part-time addition to the unit's administrative staff?

With some imagination and some cash input, the remote communities maintained by the military could be transformed into attractive places for wives and families to spend one, two, or even three years.

* * *

In Conclusion ...

The concrete ideas for change proffered in this and preceding chapters are intended as 'for instances', riders to the general thesis that military men, their families and their communities can no longer be treated as though they were 'Crown Property'. This attitude, which clings to paternalism and perpetuates undesirable 'Us and Them', civilian/military divisions, must be discredited and abandoned if genuine progress is to be made. It is vital that the problems of the military man who is also a family man be addressed, for the nation requires Armed Forces and the Armed Forces require ever more skilled men who have to serve for longer periods to amortize their training costs and to maximize use of their experience. The long-serving man will usually have a family and that family will probably subscribe to symmetrical ideals. These are not compatible with a paternalistic, authoritarian system. If the military fails to examine its relationship with families and with its own men in their capacity as family men, it will run into trouble. An antagonistic family can put great pressure upon a man to leave his Service or can cause endless problems for welfare agencies. At the time of writing, Britain has an unemployment problem—and still, a worrying large number of able men leave the military. Almost every one will cite a family reason for doing so, if asked. Should the employment situation improve, who can say how difficult it may become to retain skilled personnel?

Other people will have more and better ideas as to specific ways in which dealings with family men, their wives, children and communities can be improved. The object of this book is to point out with some degree of urgency, that the 'Crown Property' mentality espoused by the military for so long, must give way to a more sensitive and respectful approach to individuals.

The military has so much to offer, but it has always been a conservative institution, resistant to change and especially to social change. Pointless lamentations over imagined 'declining standards' and futile attempts to 'restore' them will not help the situation one bit. The Services should work out new policies to adapt to today's circumstances. If they insist on standing, Canute-like, on the shore, trying to turn back the tide of social change, they may find themselves suddenly in deep water, floundering.

Notes

Preface

1. Myna Trustrum. *Women of the Regiment*. Cambridge University Press 1984.

Chapter 1: The Military Man in a Changing Society

1. Corelli Barnett. *The Military Profession in the 1970s*. From The Armed Services and Society: Alienation, Management and Integration. Ed. J. N. Wolfe and John Erickson. Edinburgh University Press.
2. Myna Trustrum. *Women of the Regiment*. Cambridge University Press 1984.
3. Ibid.
4. Michael Young and Peter Wilmott. *The Symmetrical Family*. Routledge & Kegan Paul 1973. Penguin Books 1975.
5. *Social Trends 1985*. HMSO 1985.
6. Sar E. Levitan & Richard Belous. *What's Happening to the American Family?* John Hopkins. University Press. London 1979.
7. Rhona & Robert Rapoport. *Dual Career Families*. Penguin Books 1971.
8. A. H. Halsey. *Change in British Society*. Oxford University Press 1978.
9. Ross D. Parke. *Fathering*. Fontana Books 1981.
10. Maureen Green. *Goodbye Father*. Routledge & Kegan Paul 1976.
11. Jacques Grandmaison. *The Modern Family: Locus of Resistance or Agency of Change*. From The Family in Crisis or in Transition. Ed. Andrew Greely. The Seabury Press. New York.
12. Leonard Benson. *Fatherhood: A Sociological Perspective*. Random House.
13. Colin Hughes. *Thoroughly Modern Military. The Times*. 19 February 1985.
14. *Armed Forces Accommodation and Family Education Survey*. MOD Internal Paper.
15. Ibid.
16. *Survey of Wives of Service Personnel*. HMSO 1985.
17. *Social Trends 1985*.
18. J. Haskey. *Social Class and Socio-economic Differentials in Divorce in England and Wales*. Central Statistical Office (Population Studies 38 (1984) 419–439).
19. Machiavelli. *The Prince. 12 (44–45)*. Translation by Luigi Ricci. Revision by E. R. P. Vincent. 'Worlds Classics'. Oxford University Press 1935.

Chapter 2: Young Men Going Places

1. James Fallows. *9 to 5 and Home to Dinner – The Civilianisation of the Army*. Atlantic Monthly Vol 247 No 4 April 1981.
2. Dr Cathy Downes. *God, Queen and Country. Institutional and Occupational Trends in the British Armed Forces*. University of Melbourne 1985.

Chapter 3: Military Communities: 'The Married Patch'

1. Elizabeth Dunn. *Militant Tendencies. The Sunday Times*. February 1986.

Chapter 4: Variations on a Theme: Different Kinds of Military Community

1. Irene Fox. *Private Schools and Public Issues. The Parents View.* Macmillan 1985.
2. Ibid.
3. Ibid.
4. Royston Lambert. *The Chance of a Lifetime? A Study of Boarding Education.* Weidenfeld & Nicolson 1975.
5. Irene Fox.

Chapter 8: The Military and its Families: Which Way Forward?

1. Colonel & Mrs M. Gaffney. *The Army Wives Study 1986.* MOD Internal Paper. An excellent report which acknowledges the problem of 'attitude'. Although the authors' terms of reference did not, unfortunately, encourage much philosophical speculation, it is highly recommended reading for those with a particular interest in the problems of Army families.
2. Peter Rayner *Children of the Professionals. Social Work Today.* 30 April 1984.

Basis for Gathering Study Material by Interview

Subjects were grouped under three heads and the outline of the questionnaires put to each group is shown in the following Annexes:

ANNEX A
Young Married Couples

Subjects

Young married. Children under five years old or planning to have a family. Husband with good career prospects—a 'high flyer'.

General Background

Service.
Rank.
Wife's Occupation.
Ages.
Education and Qualifications.
Age and sex of children, if any.
Family of origin. (N.B. Father's occupation, mother's occupation, if any. Siblings.)
How and where the couple met.

Homes

What constitutes a 'home'?
Do you think you will spend any/some/most of your married life in married quarters?
At what stage, if at all, would you aim to buy a house?
Do you think at all about settling down in one locality?
How do you share household management tasks?
Spending decisions.

Paying bills.
Maintenance and repairs.
Cooking.
Shopping.
Cleaning.
Laundry.
Recreational decisions – e.g. T.V. programmes
                          Night out.
                          Holiday.

Careers

Husband's attitude to career. (Does he seem to regard it as a vocation, a profession or a job?)
His ambitions.
Husband's career decisions; do you both talk them over or does the husband take them alone?
Wife's career or job. What does, or did, she do and is it important to her?
How does she envisage her employment in the future?
How does the couple feel about the effects of mobility on a wife's employment?

Children (where applicable)

Do you think you are in any way a different style of father/mother from your own father/mother?

Tasks: Does husband . . .
    Play?
    Cuddle?
    Feed?
    Change nappies?
    Dress?
    Push pram or pushchair?
    Wash and iron clothes?
    Take to Doctor?
    Take to School?

Education (all interviewees)

How important do you consider formal education and paper qualifications?
How important is it for father to have contact with children's schools? (Parents' evenings, plays, concerts etc)
What are your opinions, if any, about boarding school education for your children?

How do you feel about the effects, if any, of separation/mobility on your children?

In what ways do you think that belonging to the Service will help you as a family?
In what ways do you think that belonging to the Service will create difficulties?

ANNEX B
Serviceman

Personal Information
    Service
    Rank
    Age
    Military or non-military family of origin?
    Qualifications
    Any occupation before entering the military
    Number and ages of children
    Mobility—has it been high or low?
    Family experience of different kinds of life style: 'camp followers,' depôt family, overseas base, boarding-school children, commuting husband, fully settled.

Postings
    Looking back over your years of married life, are there any postings which you remember with particular affection—as times of *family* stability and contentment?
    Also the converse: did any postings produce more than their fair share of *family* worries?
    (NB Age and stage of the family at the time, location, life style.)

Home
    What, to you, constitutes 'home'? (People, personal possessions, house, locality?)
    How has moving affected your family?

Absence on Duty
    Do you ever resent having to leave your family?
    Is it difficult when you return?
    How well does your family cope without you? (Include children.)

Work and Social Commitment
    Have there been occasions when work or work-related social commitments have strained family relationships? If so, have you resented the demands of the military?

Support

When the sort of problems we've been talking about arise, who do you grumble to?

To whom does your wife turn for support?

Thinking about Leaving

Have you thought seriously about leaving? If so, why? Family reasons?

Has your wife ever tried to persuade you to leave?

Serious Marital Problems

Has your marriage ever been through a particularly 'sticky' patch due to the demands of military life?

How common in your peer group have the following problems been:

Early marriage, separation and infidelity.

Young mother coping difficulties.

Money problems linked to social commitment.

Disenchantment with the military way of life.

Children's education problems.

Wives' employment problems.

Problems with alcohol.

Personal Effectiveness

Can you recollect whether family worries have ever caused you to do your job badly?

Do you feel that military duties have ever caused you to be a poor husband or father?

Changing Social Attitudes

Do you think that the outlook and attitude of service wives has changed at all over the time since you have been married?

Have your own attitudes changed?

(Note: Fewer servicemen than Service wives were interviewed, and the men displayed a greater tendency to expand on some topics—usually in response to direct questions about themselves—while being less forthcoming on others, often those questions concerning their own marriages.)

ANNEX 6
Service Wife

Personal Information

Husband's Service.

Husband's Rank.

Age.

Military or non-military family of origin?
Qualifications.
Occupation, before and after marriage.
Number and ages of children.
Mobility—How many homes in how many years of marriage.
Experience of different life styles: 'Camp followers', Depôt family, Overseas base, Boarding-school children, Commuting husband, Fully-settled.

Postings

Looking back over your years of married life, are there any postings which you remember with particular affection—as times of family stability and contentment?
Also the converse: did any postings produce more than their fair share of family worries?
(N.B. Age and stage of the family at the time, location, lifestyle.)

Home

What, to you, constitutes 'home'?
(People, personal possessions, house, locality?)
How has moving affected you? (Ties with friends, place, job—consequent loss of status, self-confidence, self-esteem? etc.)
How has moving affected your children?

Absence of Husband on Duty

What are the main difficulties which *you* face when your husband is away?
(Include readjustment to return.)
What effect, if any, do you think your husband's absences have had on your children?

Social Commitment

Do you think that the military demand to relax as a 'team' strains family relationships? Do you ever resent these social demands?

Support

When the sort of problems we've been talking about arise, who do you grumble to?
Over the years, how involved in 'official' support activities have you been? (Mess functions, Wives' activities, Children's activities.)
Which activities did you enjoy and which, if any, did you find a strain?

Thinking about Leaving

Have you ever tried to influence your husband to leave the Service because of the effect which military life was having on the family?
Can you see this happening in the future?

Serious Marital Problems

Has your marriage ever been through a particularly 'sticky' patch due to the demands of military life?

How common in your peer-group have the following problems been:

Early marriage, separation and infidelity.

Young mother coping difficulties.

Money problems linked to social commitment.

Disenchantment with the military way of life.

Children's education.

Wives' employment.

Alcohol.

Personal Effectiveness

Have there been occasions when the demands of military life have caused you:

(1) Serious Depression.

(2) To miss out on job or career opportunities?

Changing Social Attitudes

Do you think that the outlook and attitude of Service wives has changed at all over the time since you married?

Have your own attitudes changed?

Appendix II

Guide to Equivalent Ranks in the Army, the Royal Navy and the Royal Air Force

ARMY	NAVY	RAF
Private (Trooper, Gunner, etc.)	Ordinary Seaman	Aircraftman
Lance-Corporal/Lance-Bombardier	Able Seaman	Leading Aircraftman
Corporal/Bombardier	Leading Seaman	Senior Aircraftman Corporal/Junior Technician
Sergeant	Petty Officer	Sergeant
Quartermaster Sergeant/Staff Sergeant	Chief Petty Officer	Flight Sergeant/Chief Technician
Warrant Officer 2nd Class/Squadron Battery or Company Sergeant Major		Master Aircrew/Warrant Officer
Warrant Officer 1st Class/ Regimental Sergeant Major	Fleet Chief Petty Officer	
Second Lieutenant	Sub-Lieutenant	Pilot Officer
Lieutenant		Flying Officer
Captain	Lieutenant	Flight Lieutenant
Major	Lieutenant-Commander	Squadron Leader
Lieutenant Colonel	Commander	Wing Commander
Colonel	Captain	Group Captain
Brigadier	Commodore	Air Commodore
Major General	Rear-Admiral	Air Vice-Marshal
Lieutenant General	Vice-Admiral	Air Marshal
General	Admiral	Air Chief Marshal
Field Marshal	Admiral of the Fleet	Marshal of the RAF

Recommended for Further Reading

Barker, Dennis. (1981) *Soldiering On – An Unofficial Portrait of the British Army*. Andre Deutsch.
Beail, Nigel and McGuire, Jacqueline. (Ed.) (1982) *Fathers. Psychological Perspectives*. Junction Books Ltd.
Benson, Leonard. (1968) *Fatherhood: A Sociological Perspective*. Random House.
Berger, Brigitte and Peter. (1983) *The War Over the Family. Capturing the Middle Ground*. Hutchinson & Co.
Braddon, Russell. (1977) *All the Queen's Men*. Hamish Hamilton.
Crane, Jonathan. (1984) *Submarine*. British Broadcasting Corporation.
Davie, Ronald. (1972) 'What is a Good Family?' *National Children's Bureau, Conference Papers*.
Dixon, Norman. (1976) *On the Psychology of Military Incompetence*. Jonathan Cape.
Downes, Cathy. (1985) *God, Queen and Country. Institutional and Occupational Trends in the British Armed Forces*. University of Melbourne, Victoria, Australia.
Eichenbaum, Luise and Orbach, Susie. (1983) *What do Women Want?* Michael Joseph.
Enloe, Cynthia. (1983) *The Militarisation of Women's Lives*. Pluto Press.
Fallows, James. (1981) '9 to 5 and Home for Dinner – the Civilianisation of the Army.' *Atlantic Monthly* Vol. 247 No. 4 *April issue. 1981*.
Farmer, Mary. (1979) *The Family*. Longman.
Farwell, Byron. (1978) *For Queen and Country*. Allen, Lane.
Fox, Irene. (1985) *Private Schools and Public Issues. The Parents' View*. Macmillan.
Greeley, Andrew. (Ed.) *The Modern Family: Locus of Resistance or Agency of Change*. The Seabury Press. N. York.
Green, Maureen. (1976) *Goodbye Father*. Routledge & Kegan Paul.
Halsey, A. H. (1981) *Change in British Society*. Oxford University Press.
Hilton, Frank. (1983) *The Paras*. British Broadcasting Corporation.
Leviton, Sar A. and Belous, Richard. (1979) *What's Happening to the American Family?* John Hopkins University Press.
Margiotta, Frank. (Ed.) (1978) *The Changing World of the American Military*. Westview Press.
Murray Parkes, Colin. (1974) *Bereavement*. Tavistock Publications.
Newson, Elizabeth. (1972) 'Towards an Understanding of the Parental Role.' *National Children's Bureau, Conference Papers*.
Owen, Charles. (1975) *No More Heroes – The Royal Navy in the Twentieth Century*. George, Allen & Unwin.
Parke, Ross. (1981) *Fathering*. Fontana.
Parker, Tony. (1985) *Soldier, Soldier*. William Heinemann Ltd.
Reader, W. J. (1966) *Professional Men: The Rise of the Professional Classes in the Nineteenth Century*. Weidenfeld & Nicolson.
Rapoport, Rhona and Robert. (1971) *Dual Career Families*. Penguin.
Sabine, John. (1977) *British Defence Policy in a Changing World*. Croom, Holm.
Sexton, Patricia. (1970) *The Feminised Male*. Unwin.
Strong, Colin. (1983) *Fighter Pilot*. British Broadcasting Corporation.
Trustrum, Myna. (1984) *Women of the Regiment*. Cambridge University Press.
Young, Michael and Willmott, Peter. (1973) *The Symmetrical Family*. Routledge & Kegan Paul.

Index